SpringerBriefs in Education

We are delighted to announce SpringerBriefs in Education, an innovative product type that combines elements of both journals and books. Briefs present concise summaries of cutting-edge research and practical applications in education. Featuring compact volumes of 50 to 125 pages, the SpringerBriefs in Education allow authors to present their ideas and readers to absorb them with a minimal time investment. Briefs are published as part of Springer's eBook Collection. In addition, Briefs are available for individual print and electronic purchase.

SpringerBriefs in Education cover a broad range of educational fields such as: Science Education, Higher Education, Educational Psychology, Assessment & Evaluation, Language Education, Mathematics Education, Educational Technology, Medical Education and Educational Policy.

SpringerBriefs typically offer an outlet for:

- An introduction to a (sub)field in education summarizing and giving an overview of theories, issues, core concepts and/or key literature in a particular field
- A timely report of state-of-the art analytical techniques and instruments in the field of educational research
- A presentation of core educational concepts
- An overview of a testing and evaluation method
- A snapshot of a hot or emerging topic or policy change
- An in-depth case study
- A literature review
- A report/review study of a survey
- An elaborated thesis

Both solicited and unsolicited manuscripts are considered for publication in the SpringerBriefs in Education series. Potential authors are warmly invited to complete and submit the Briefs Author Proposal form. All projects will be submitted to editorial review by editorial advisors.

SpringerBriefs are characterized by expedited production schedules with the aim for publication 8 to 12 weeks after acceptance and fast, global electronic dissemination through our online platform SpringerLink. The standard concise author contracts guarantee that:

- an individual ISBN is assigned to each manuscript
- each manuscript is copyrighted in the name of the author
- the author retains the right to post the pre-publication version on his/her website or that of his/her institution

More information about this series at http://www.springer.com/series/8914

Anat Even Zahav · Orit Hazzan

Risk Management of Education Systems

The Case of STEM Education in Israel

Springer

Anat Even Zahav
Technion-Israel Institute of Technology
Haifa
Israel

Orit Hazzan
Technion-Israel Institute of Technology
Haifa
Israel

ISSN 2211-1921 ISSN 2211-193X (electronic)
SpringerBriefs in Education
ISBN 978-3-319-51983-8 ISBN 978-3-319-51984-5 (eBook)
DOI 10.1007/978-3-319-51984-5

Library of Congress Control Number: 2016962049

Printed on acid-free paper

This Springer imprint is published by Springer Nature
The registered company is Springer International Publishing AG
The registered company address is: Gewerbestrasse 11, 6330 Cham, Switzerland

Preface

Risk Management—Context and Rationale

In the Global Competitiveness Report 2012–2013 of the World Economic Forum, Israel ranked third in the world for its innovative ability, but only 89th for the achievements of its students in mathematics and science (The Global Competitiveness Report, 2012–2013). In light of these findings, the need arises to improve STEM education in Israel.

One way to improve the performance of education systems is by the implementation of risk management process. Risk management principles can be applied to any organization regardless its size, activity, or sector (ISO Guide73, 2009). However, so far it has not been carried out for national education systems. The following questions are raised: Can risk management be implemented for national education systems? If it can, how? If not, why?

In this Brief, we attempt to answer these questions, illustrating the need and methodology for such a process. Specifically, we focus on risk management of STEM education in Israel. This topic is worth examination for two main reasons. First, the increased attention the STEM subjects get recently world-wide due to the realization that these subjects are needed for both individuals' and nations' wealth, prosperity, and ongoing development and growth (see, e.g., Prepare and Inspire: K-12 Education in Science, Technology, Engineering, and Math (STEM) for America's Future, 2010). Second, specifically, with respect to Israel, the STEM subjects form the basis for its hi-tech sector, which is one of Israel's key economic engines; therefore, STEM education should be treated as a strategic risk.

We lay out the implementation of a risk management method for the identification of the challenges of STEM education in Israel and for outlining a response plan for coping with these challenges. We also assert the present common acknowledgment that education should not concern only the education sector, but rather all sectors should be involved in its promotion in general and the promotion of STEM education in particular. Therefore, we suggest that this Brief is relevant for anyone who is interested in STEM education, from all sectors—government and local authorities (the first sector), industry (the second sector), and nonprofit NGOs, including academia (the third sector).

Brief Organization

The Brief is organized as follows.

Chapter 1 describes education systems in the world in the context of STEM education, addressing characteristics of successful education systems. As we shall see, some of the accepted characteristics of successful education systems are considered also in the industry as characteristics that foster successful organizations.

Chapter 2 presents four basic concepts of strategic analysis—a strategic analysis model, SWOT analysis, Delphi method and risk management—as they are used in the business sector, as well as their adaptation for the analysis of the case of STEM education.

Chapter 3 reviews the domain of STEM education in Israel, including a historical overview, current reforms, and contemporary trends and emphasis. It also describes the research process that guided the risk management process, presented in this Brief.

Chapter 4 describes the risk identification process of STEM education in Israel by SWOT analysis. It outlines seven risk categories of 43 risk factors, based on the analysis of bureaucratic-professional conflicts and barriers in implementing changes in education systems.

Chapter 5 presents the rating of the 43 risk factors of STEM education in Israel identified in Phase A (Chap. 4). These risk factors were rated by three levels of severity (high, medium, and low) (Mikes and Kaplan 2014). This phase also emphasizes *strategic risks* which endanger the objectives of the organization in general and in our case—the objectives of STEM education.

Chapter 6 lays out a response plan for the strategic risks. Thirteen courses of action are proposed: Five actions are internal to the education system and eight courses of action involve cross-sector cooperation with stakeholders form all sectors in Israel.

Chapter 7 presents our reflection on the Israeli case and lays out several meta-guidelines how to tackle risks with which education systems face. We highlight guidelines, such as diversity and inclusion as well as the use of knowledge generated outside the education field.

Haifa, Israel

Anat Even Zahav
Orit Hazzan

Reference

ISO Guide 73. (2009). *Risk management—Vocabulary: A Collection of Terms and Definitions Relating to the Management of Risk.* International Organization for Standardization. http://www.iso.org/iso/home/standards/iso31000.htm

Mikes, A., & Kaplan, R. S. (2014). *Towards a Contingency Theory of Enterprise Risk Management*. Harvard Business School.

Prepare and Inspire: K-12 Education in Science, Technology, Engineering, and Math (STEM) for America's Future (2010). https://www.whitehouse.gov/sites/default/files/microsites/ostp/pcast-stemed-report.pdf

The Global Competitiveness Report (2012–2013). Country Profile Highlights. http://www3.weforum.org/docs/CSI/2012-13/GCR_CountryHighlights_2012-13.pdf

Terminology

This section presents the terminology related to STEM—Science, Technology, Engineering and Mathematics—education in Israel, for which the risk management process described in this Brief was applied.

Divisions of the Ministry of Education Related to STEM Education in Secondary Schools

The subject matters taught in Israeli schools are divided into two divisions. With respect to the STEM subjects, the classical science field is affiliated to one division (A below) and the other subjects to another division (B below).

A. *Science education*

- The following subjects are managed by the Pedagogical Secretary of the Ministry of Education: Mathematics, Physics, Chemistry, Biology, Environmental science, Earth sciences, Agricultural sciences, and Science and Technology For All.
- Among them, the following subjects provide a scientific and technological excellence matriculation diploma when studied on the advanced level: Mathematics, Physics, Chemistry, Biology, and Computer science (which belongs to the Science and Technology Division).
- Mathematics is a compulsory subject for all students and is taught on different levels.

B. *Technology education*

- The technology subjects are managed by the Science and Technology Division of the Ministry of Education.
- The Science and Technology Division includes three tracks:

- *The engineering track* includes the following courses: Software engineering, Mechanical engineering, Electrical engineering, Computer engineering, and Biotechnology. This track requires the highest learning requirements in the technology education division and it enables to finish high school with an excellence diploma in science and technology.
- *The technology track* includes the following courses: Energy control systems, Computerized production systems, Construction and architecture, Industrial management, Design arts, Communication technology, Media and publishing, Marine systems, and more. *Technology education* prepares the students to work in hi-tech environments. It educates the students to use knowledge effectively to find solutions to new problems with which they face.
- *The occupational track* includes the following courses: Business management, Health systems, Tourism and Leisure, and more.

Technology Education Under the Supervision of Other Ministries

In addition to the schools that are supervised by the Ministry of Education, other ministries manage schools for youth in ages 15–18, who, in most cases, did not succeed in the schools which belong to the Ministry of Education. These schools offer the following courses: Cooking, Inspected aircraft, Computer graphics, Maintenance of PCs and networks, Auto electronics, Auto mechanics, and more.[1]

These schools supervise by The Ministry of Economy and Industry. The Ministry of Education started a long-term process of adopting these schools so that all Israel children will study under one roof.

In this Brief, *vocational education* refers to the technology track and the occupational track (supervised either by the Ministry of Education or by the Ministry of Economy & Industry). *Vocational education* teaches practice-oriented subjects and technical skills and trains the students to be effective workers in a specific technical area. These studies include tools and machinery, materials and their properties, knowledge management processes and manufacturing practices.

[1]Source: The Ministry of Economy and Industry.
http://economy.gov.il/Employment/ManpowerTraining/YouthTraining/SchoolsAndCourses/Pages/megamot.aspx.

Contents

1 STEM Education in the World 1
1.1 Introduction 1
1.2 Characteristics of Successful Education Systems 2
1.2.1 The Teaching Profession 3
1.2.2 Diversity 4
1.3 Summary 5
References 5

2 Strategic Analysis 7
2.1 A Strategic Analysis Model 7
2.2 SWOT Analysis 8
2.3 Delphi Method 9
2.4 Risk Management 10
2.5 Summary 14
References 15

3 STEM Education in Israel: A Case Study 17
3.1 STEM Education in Israel: Past and Present 17
3.2 Research Framework 19
3.2.1 Research Methodology 19
3.2.2 Research Participants 20
3.2.3 Research Tools 21
3.2.4 Research Process 22
3.3 Summary 23
References 24

4 Phase A: Risk Identification—Identification of Risk Categories by SWOT Analysis of STEM Education in Israel 25
4.1 Conflicts and Barriers 25
4.1.1 The Bureaucratic-Professional Conflict 25
4.1.2 Barriers in Change Processes 27

4.2 Seven Risk Categories 28
4.2.1 Risk Category: Sectors in STEM Education 29
4.2.2 Risk Category: Teachers—Opportunities, Training, and Social Status 36
4.2.3 Risk Category: Curriculum of STEM Subjects 38
4.2.4 Risk Category: Study Sequences—School, Higher Education, Military, Labor Market 40
4.2.5 Risk Category: Management of STEM Education 42
4.2.6 Risk Category: Social Perceptions 44
4.2.7 Risk Category: National Programs in STEM Education 46
4.3 Summary 47
References 47

5 Phase B: Risk Rating 49
5.1 The "Risk Management—Risk Rating" Questionnaire 49
5.1.1 The "Risk Management—Risk Rating" Questionnaire Formulation 50
5.1.2 The "Risk Management—Risk Rating" Questionnaire Distribution 51
5.1.3 The "Risk Management—Risk Rating" Questionnaire Analysis 51
5.2 Finding: Risks Rating—Identification of Significant Risks for STEM Education in Israel 56
5.2.1 The Scores of the 43 Risk Factors 57
5.2.2 Grouping the Risk Factors by Three Levels of Severity: High, Medium, and Low 58
5.2.3 Risk Categories Rating by Their Severity Impact on STEM Education in Israel 61
5.3 Summary 62
References 62

6 Phase C: Risk Response 63
6.1 Introduction to the Response Phase: Operational Risks, Strategic Risks, and External Risks 63
6.2 Response Plan 66
6.3 Four Strategic Risks and 13 Courses of Action 72
6.3.1 Strategic Risk 1: The Social Status of the Teaching Profession in Israel 75
6.3.2 Strategic Risk 2: Public Image of Technology Education 79
6.3.3 Strategic Risk 3: Negative Perceptions Regarding Science Subjects 81
6.3.4 Strategic Risk 4: Sectoral Gaps 83

6.4 Cross-Sector Collaboration in Risk Management of STEM Education 85
6.5 Summary 87
References 87

7 What Can STEM Education Systems in the World Learn from the Israeli Case? 89
7.1 Meta-Practices of Risk Management 89
7.2 Summary 91
Reference 91

List of Figures

Figure 5.1 Distribution of the respondents by sector 51
Figure 5.2 Averages and standard deviations of risks factors 57
Figure 5.3 Risk categories ranking 61
Figure 6.1 Response plan for risk management of STEM education in Israel 71
Figure 6.2 Mapping of STEM education risks in Israel 72
Figure 6.3 Dealing with risks of STEM education in Israel—Education system and cooperation with stakeholders 75

List of Tables

Table 4.1 Risk categories, conflicts, and barriers: the 43 risk factors of STEM education in Israel 30
Table 4.2 Risk categories, conflicts and barriers 33
Table 4.3 Sectors in STEM education—barriers and risk factors 34
Table 4.4 Teachers—conflicts, barriers, and risk factors 38
Table 4.5 Curriculum—risk factors and the profession perception conflict 39
Table 4.6 Study sequences—the procedural barrier and risk factors 41
Table 4.7 Management of STEM education—conflicts, barriers, and risk factors 42
Table 4.8 Social perceptions—barriers and risk factors 46
Table 4.9 National programs—barriers and risk factors 46
Table 5.1 Fifteen risk factors with high severity level 52
Table 5.2 Eighteen risk factors with medium severity level 53
Table 5.3 Ten risk factors with low severity level 55
Table 5.4 Criteria for selecting risk severity levels 58
Table 5.5 Number of risk factors by their categories and severity levels 60
Table 6.1 Ten risks of STEM education in Israel 67
Table 6.2 Courses of action for mitigating the strategic risks 73

Chapter 1
STEM Education in the World

Abstract In this chapter, we describe education systems in the world in the context of STEM education, addressing characteristics of successful education systems as well as how these characteristics are related to the business sector. As we shall see, some of the accepted characteristics of successful education systems are accepted also in the industry as characteristics that foster successful organizations. We highlight this aspect since this Brief delivers a similar message with respect to risk management; that is, risk management can be applied for education systems as it is applied in the business system. At the same time, we should remember, though, that any such application should be considered carefully before applied on a full scale.

Keywords STEM education · Risk management · Future generations · Economic success · Successful education system · Job market · Teaching profession · Finnish education system · Canadian education system · Diversity

1.1 Introduction

STEM education gets recently a lot of attention around the world due to several reasons.

(1) It is well recognized that the STEM subjects are essential for the success of nations' future generations. Furthermore, while it is acknowledged that many professions will disappear in the near future,[1] it is commonly agreed that professions which are based on the STEM subjects will remain relevant and their importance may even increase. Specifically, while it is understood that the professions that will probably disappear in the near future will be replaced by automatic systems, it is also acknowledged that the science and engineering disciplines cannot be automated since they involve creativity and complexity

[1]See, for example, http://www.businessinsider.com/15-jobs-that-are-quickly-disappearing-2015-10/#printing-worker-1 and http://www.forbes.com/pictures/lmj45ighg/top-20-disappearing-jobs/#3197c69a6589.

A. Even Zahav and O. Hazzan, *Risk Management of Education Systems*, SpringerBriefs in Education, DOI 10.1007/978-3-319-51984-5_1

that (at least at this stage) can be expressed only by the human mind. Thus, by fostering and enabling the future generations to study the STEM subjects, nations, in fact, ensure the future prosperity of their countries both on the individual level and the national level.

(2) On the individual level, basic knowledge in the STEM subjects is needed either for the personal life as well as for the individuals' professional development. Specifically, in private lives, people need basic STEM-related skills to manage information, decide about economic strategies, and manipulate the data overflow that we all face on a daily basis. In our professional lives, knowledge in the STEM domains enables mobility (a characteristic of the future job market) either within the same industry and geographical area or between sectors (government, industry, and nonprofit NGOs) and geographical boarders.

Due to the importance attributed to STEM education, it is not surprising that recent educational reforms focus on the STEM subjects.

For example, President Barack Obama, in the third Annual White House Science Fair that took place in April 2013 said that "One of the things that I've been focused on as President is how we create an all-hands-on-deck approach to science, technology, engineering, and math… We need to make this a priority to train an army of new teachers in these subject areas, and to make sure that all of us as a country are lifting up these subjects for the respect that they deserve."[2] More recently, the focus is placed on computer science education. The target is to spread computer science education to more students in all ages[3] in order to close the shortage of human resources in this subject and to prepare the next generation for the future workforce. Obama's initiative of computer science education clearly reflects

- the tight connection between STEM education and nation's job markets, and
- the responsibility of education systems to think forward about the professional development of its future graduates.

1.2 Characteristics of Successful Education Systems

This section presents factors that are recognized as characteristics of success education systems in the world and their implications for STEM education. We highlight their relevance and expression in the industry sector in order to support one of the main ideas illustrated in this Brief. According to this idea, it is possible, and sometimes recommended, to apply strategic methods which are commonly used in the industry—in our case, risk management—for education systems as well.

---

[2]See: https://www.whitehouse.gov/issues/education/k-12/educate-innovate.

[3]See: http://www.theatlantic.com/education/archive/2016/02/obamas-push-for-computer-science-education/459276/.

We focus on the human side of education addressing the teaching profession (Sect. 1.2.1) and diversity (Sect. 1.2.2). These characteristics deliver the message that each teacher and pupil has a unique individualism that the education system should support by promoting autonomy, teamwork, and knowledge sharing.

1.2.1 The Teaching Profession

"The quality of an education system cannot exceed the quality of its teachers." states McKinsey Report (2007). Indeed, the roles and status of STEM teachers was found to be one of the major risks with which STEM education in Israel faces and accordingly, the response plan widely addresses it.

Specifically, the perspective described in this Brief bridges the two approaches toward education systems in general and the teaching profession in particular, as described in Hargreaves and Fullan (2012). The first is a *business capital* approach, according to which the purpose of public education is to yield a short-term profit with quick ROI (returns for investments). They further argue that this approach fosters the idea that public education should be considered as a potential market for technology. The opposite approach toward teaching is a *professional capital* approach, according to which teaching is hard and requires special skills with an ongoing professional development. The idea presented in this Brief bridges these two approaches and thus, fits Hargreaves and Fullan's approach, who advocate that teachers should be considered as nation builders (2012, p. 185).

Finland is a good example for this approach, whose education system is considered as one of the best education systems in the world. Sahlberg (2011) describes the process that led to this status, as well as its characteristics. Among the important factors, on which the process relied, are teacher characteristics, as well as the public attitude toward the profession of teaching and teachers' working conditions.

Teamwork is one of the basic principles of Finnish education. Teamwork enables the Finnish education system to turn the profession of teaching from an 'industrial' profession, that is based on imparting a certain amount of material within a certain number of hours to many pupils as possible, into a more 'clinical' profession, in which each student receives individual attention according to his or her special needs (throughout the whole spectrum of excellence). In addition, in Finland, the teachers determine how to achieve the objectives set by the education system and develop the curriculum accordingly; the education system just provides them with the required means to do that (Sahlberg 2011). This approach is based on teacher autonomy, which is one of the highest human needs, that when applied to the work place, is expressed in high motivation (Maslow 1943). It delivers the message that teachers are professionals who can perform their jobs successfully without any supervision. Thus, teachers in Finland are motivated to achieve the goals they set for themselves with respect to each of their pupils. As a side effect, this approach, which eliminates the supervision tier and minimizes administration and bureaucracy, enables to improve resource utilization.

Furthermore, in Finland as a nation, this approach to education is manifested also in other social characteristics, such as small social gaps and the value that grants everyone the same right for education.

1.2.2 Diversity

Diversity is a value that many companies foster in order to increase their success (Hazzan and Dubinsky 2006). Diversity can be expressed in different ways, such as nationalities, genders, minorities, cultures, and life styles. Diversity can also be expressed with respect to internal characteristics, such as worldviews, hobbies, skills, thinking styles, etc.

In the context of education, diversity is usually promoted by a multicultural perspective, which means "a set of strategies and materials in education that were developed to assist teachers when responding to the many issues created by the rapidly changing demographics of their students."[4]

Canada illustrates very clearly this approach by the ways its education system embraces multiculturalism and educates its immigrant students. "Canada was one of only a few countries in which immigrant students had access to equal or greater resources than native-born students. Specifically, student/teacher ratios, physical infrastructure, classroom climate, and teacher morale were on average higher for the immigrant students sampled than for native students [...] immigrant students are for the most part placed into classes with native students in English and French." (OECD 2010, p. 71). The story of the Canadian education system is presented in details in Fullan 2014. Fullan (2014) also highlights the autonomy (discussed in the previous section) given to teachers, principals, schools, and districts in determining their goals and the ways to achieve them.

This approach to education contrasts the structure of the Israeli education system in which different education systems exist for each social group (general, religious, ultraorthodox and Arab), which clearly conflicts the value of diversity, inclusion, and multiculturalism. This structure leads to a situation in which (a) some subjects are studied on different levels and depth in the different sectors; (b) diversity is blocked and students from the different sectors almost do not meet each other; and (c) national values and targets are hardly promoted.

In particular, this structure of the education system leads to a situation in which the STEM subjects are not studied on the same level by all social groups. As a result, the participation and contribution to Israel economic development and growth, as a leading science and technological center (Sensor and Singer 2009), is blocked for some parts of the population. Furthermore, these differences lead to

[4]*Source* https://en.wikipedia.org/wiki/Multicultural_education.

social gaps, inequity, and differences in individual's mobility. As we shall see later in this Brief, the structure of the Israeli education system (with its consequences) was identified in the risk identification stage of our study (Chap. 4).

1.3 Summary

As we shall see in the continuation of this Brief, the above analysis is highly relevant for the risk management process applied for STEM education in Israel. Israel has a central education system (which blocks teachers' and principals' autonomy) and diversity is not widely fostered. Accordingly, the response stage (Chap. 6) directly addresses these characteristics. It is important to note, though, that more and more voices in Israel push currently toward the assimilation of changes in the education system in the spirit of the characteristics described in this chapter.

Gale (2015) delivers a similar message: "Since risk impacts our lives in so many ways, it is not surprising that many education systems and researchers are looking for ways to embed risk assessment and management and risk-based decision-making into the K-12 school system." (p. 67).

References

Fullan, M. (2014). *Big-city School Reforms: Lessons from New York, Toronto, and London.* Teachers College Press.

Gale, L. (2015). Risk education A worldview analysis of what is present and could be, *The Mathematics Enthusiast*, vol. 12, no. 1, 2 & 3, pp. 62–84.

Hargreaves, A., & Fullan, M. (2012). *Professional Capital: Transforming Teaching in Every School.* Teachers College Press.

Hazzan, O., & Dubinsky, Y. (2006). Can diversity in global software development be enhanced by agile software development?, the *Global Software Development for the Practitioner* workshop, *Proceedings of ICSE (International Conference of Software Engineering)*, Shanghai, China, pp. 58–61.

Maslow, A. H. (1943). The Hierarchy of Needs: A Theory of Human Motivation, *Psychological Review*, 50(4), 370–396.

McKinsey Report (2007). *How the world's best performing education systems come out on top.* https://mckinseyonsociety.com/downloads/reports/Education/Worlds_School_Systems_Final.pdf.

OECD. (2010). *Strong Performers and Successful Reformers in Education: Lessons from PISA for the United States.* OECD publishing. http://www.oecd.org/pisa/pisaproducts/46580959.pdf.

Sahlberg, P. (2011). *Finnish Lessons*, the series of school reform.

Sensor, D., & Singer, S. (2009). *Start-up Nation: The Story of Israel's Economic Miracle*, Twelve.

Chapter 2
Strategic Analysis

Abstract In this chapter, we present four basic concepts of strategic analysis as they are used in the business sector, as well as their adaptation for the case of STEM education. The four concepts are: a strategic analysis model, SWOT analysis, Delphi Method, and Risk Management.

Keywords Strategic analysis model · SWOT analysis · Delphi method · STEM education · Risk management

2.1 A Strategic Analysis Model

A business strategy addresses organizational objectives and the examination of actions needed for their actualization. The actions are based on the available resources and the evaluation of the internal as well as the external environments in which the organization operates (Nag et al. 2007).

This Brief describes a study which implemented a strategic analysis for STEM education in general and specially for the secondary school STEM education in Israel; accordingly, it refers to the strategic actions that should be taken in order to improve the achievements in STEM education on both the individual level and the national level. The study implemented a strategic planning process as is used in business organizations.

The model we used is based on three stages (described below based on Godet 2008) which sometimes, are intertwined in each other.

A. **Pre-active—preliminary thinking—phase**. At this stage, the organization's vision, which describes the desirable future reality of the organization, is determined. In order to foster an organizational change and to plan the desirable future changes, a wide variety of diverse ideas related to the future of the organization are suggested at this stage. Specifically, possible future scenarios are constructed based on experts' insights, both from within and outside the organization, who work together on forecasting the future of the organization and identifying threats and opportunities. The thinking on and planning for the future prepares the organization

A. Even Zahav and O. Hazzan, *Risk Management of Education Systems*, SpringerBriefs in Education, DOI 10.1007/978-3-319-51984-5_2

toward the implementation of the actions that should be taken, motivate the employees, and provide a meaningful direction towards the future.

B. **Proactive—preparation for the future—phase**. In this stage, based on the analysis of the targets identified in the previous phase, the strategy how to achieve these targets is selected by a small team, comprises usually of managers. In addition, at this stage, the organization lays out its desirable reality, as well as its desirable quantitative measurable achievements for the future.

Then, under uncertainty conditions, several scenarios are created, which describe how to achieve the desirable change. Among the possible scenarios, one scenario is selected. This scenario should layout a flexible strategy that has the potential to exploit opportunities for the promotion of the organization's targets.

C. **Appropriation—task-oriented—phase**. At this stage, the change process is launched and promoted by a collective effort of all the employees of the organization. Specifically, strategic moves and detailed courses of action are determined for the realization of the vision and of the strategy formulated in the previous phases.

2.2 SWOT Analysis

SWOT—Strength, Weaknesses, Opportunities, and Threats—analysis is a methodological examination of the environment in which an organization operates. It is based on the examination of (a) internal characteristics of the organization (strengths and weaknesses) and (b) characteristics of the external environment of the organization (opportunities and threats). SWOT analysis allows the organization choosing operational strategies that foster its strengths and opportunities and protect it from its weaknesses and threats (Barney 1995).

Though the origin of SWOT analysis is at the business sector, it has been used also for the analysis of public sector organizations, e.g., schools and hospitals (Rego and Nunes 2010). For example, in the field of education, institutions of higher education carried out SWOT analysis for the evaluation of educational initiatives, such as the integration of information technologies (Sabbaghi and Vaidyanathan 2004).

SWOT analysis was applied in the case presented in this Brief for the identification of risks that the system of STEM education in Israel should prepare itself to face with (see Chap. 4). In our case, risks represent

- *conflicts* STEM *teachers* face while working in the education system;
- *barriers* with which *other stakeholders* of STEM education (representatives of the education system, academia, industry, military, and NGOs) face when they wish to promote changes and reforms in the education system.

2.3 Delphi Method

Delphi Method is based on expert evaluation of the topic under discussion. The process takes place in several rounds, in each of them a set of questions is answered by a group of experts. The Delphi procedure was first introduced by Olaf Helmer (1966) and included the following steps (usually called rounds):

- First round
  - Gathering a group of experts from the said field
  - Presentation of a set of questions about future trends to each expert separately
  - Each expert answers the questions individually and confidentially without any direct contact with the other experts.

This stage is usually implemented by interviews or questionnaires, which, in most cases, include open questions relevant to the study. The participants are asked to identify topics that will be discussed in the next rounds.

- Second round
  - The experts' answers gathered in the first round are presented to each expert, who is now asked to express his or her opinion about each of them.

Sometimes, a Delphi survey also included participants who are not considered experts in the field. Hussler et al. (2011) argue that heterogeneity is important, even if it slows down the process of reaching an agreement. Participant's heterogeneity and diversity bring up a variety of opinions, elevate opinions which are not considered as a main stream, and avoid the bias that can occur if only experts participate in the survey.

- Additional rounds take place in a similar manner until an agreement with respect to the desirable directions is reached.

The working assumption is that each round decreases the level of disagreement between the experts and eventually it is possible to formulate a strategy which is agreed upon all experts. The Delphi method attempts to avoid group thinking in which one expert opinion affects the other experts' perspective as it sometimes happens during brainstorming sessions (Linstone and Turoff 1975).

Delphi surveys are implemented in different research fields. Here are three examples.

- **Science policy**. Butts et al. (1978) describe a study which aimed to rate topics relevant to science education research in order to recommend topics for academic research. A large group of experts, who judged the topics and expressed different views, prioritized the topics by a Delphi survey.
- **Future forecasts, mainly technological forecast**. Since 1992, the Japanese National Institute of Science and Technology Policy (NISTEP) has been conducting large-scale surveys to identify medium to long-term directions for a

broad range of science and technology fields. For the ninth survey (2010), NISTEP combined three methods of Delphi, scenario and workshops, to form a vision of the "ideal" society and then study science, technology, and social systems that can help realize the vision.[1]
- **Software projects**. Nakatsu and Iacovo (2009) present a study that ranked possible risks for software projects that can be outsourced to organizations either within the country or abroad.

The original Delphi procedure, as was presented by Helmer (1966), has been changed significantly since then, and today, the Delphi method is implemented in a variety of ways. Therefore, Delphi surveys may differ in their different characteristics, such as the sample size—the number of experts who participate in the survey, and the number of rounds carried out till an agreement is achieved (usually, the first round aims to identify the factors relevant for discussion and additional two rounds are applied for their rating).

However, several features of the Delphi survey are always implemented: anonymity among participants; participants' feedbacks between rounds; attempt to reach consensus among participants; and use of open and closed questionnaires (Rowe and Wright 2011; Hussler et al. 2011; Hasson and Keeney 2011).

In the case described in this Brief, the Delphi method was used in the three phases of the strategic analysis process of STEM education in Israel. It included experts from five stakeholder groups, who have different expertise and interests. However, the importance attributed to the different attitudes of all participants enabled to lay out a comprehensive picture related to risk management of STEM education in Israel.

2.4 Risk Management

Risk is an internal or external event that has the potential to affect the implementation of the organizational strategy and the achievement of the objectives it sets for the future. The risk severity level is determined according to its (a) likelihood—the probability of its realization and (b) impact—the damage that the risk realization can cause (ISO Guide73 2009). The event, that is, the risk realization, may deviate the organization from achieving its desired orientation, either positively (upside) by enabling the organization to exhaust an opportunity, or negatively (downside), by threatening the achievement of the desired results.

The following events are commonly conceived as risks for different kinds of organizations: natural disasters, security holes (e.g., cyber-attacks), shortage or failures of human resources, financial crisis, unstable business environments, and project failures. On the one hand, in the field of accidents and safety at work, for example, only events that have negative consequences are considered as risks, and

[1]See http://www.nistep.go.jp/en/?page_id=56.

therefore, risk management as the field of safety focuses solely on the prevention of damage and the reduction of the intensity of the risk impacts. On the other hand, events which are recognized as an opportunity for the organization reflect a positive future. For example, an unexpected business opportunity may evolve as a result of a change introduced into the tax policy that may enable the organization to expand its markets.

Risks are classified in different ways, e.g., by different organizational concerns: strategic risks, financial risks, operational risks, political risks, and hazard risks (related to facilities or human lives) (IRM 2002). Based on Mikes and Kaplan's (2014) terminology, our examination categorized risks according to three resources: operational risks, strategic risks, and external (political and financial) risks (see Chap. 6).

Bruckner et al. (2001, in Hosseinzadehdastak and Underdown 2012) defines risk management as follows:

> Risk management refers to strategies, methods and supporting tools to identify, and control risk to an acceptable level. Additionally, all events that may prevent an organization from realizing its ambitions, plans, and goals are known as **risks**. In other words, **risks are potential problems that might happen**. As a result, identifying risks, assessing them, and estimating their impacts can help to mitigate negative their effects (p. 2).

Bruckner et al.'s definition (2001, in Hosseinzadehdastak and Underdown 2012) has been adopted for our research. Specifically, in the process of risk management, we used methods and tools to identify and control risks; e.g., SWOT analysis was applied for the risk identification. Thus, the identified risks represent weaknesses and threats for STEM education in Israel, that their existence in the future endanger the desired achievements of STEM education (for example, the need to increase the number of high school graduates in the STEM subjects on the highest level and, respectively, the number of qualified STEM teachers). The risk rating according to their severity level led to the formulation of a response plan which lays out thirteen courses of action to alleviate (mitigate) the negative impact of the highly ranked risks, in order to reduce the severity of their impact on STEM education in Israel (see Chap. 6).

In the process of risk management in the business sector, organizations adopt practices and methods in accordance with changes occurring in their internal and external environments. Therefore, risk management is an ongoing process. Though organizations and companies choose different risk management techniques which are suitable for their professional activities, a review of the relevant literature shows that organizations adopt a similar process of risk management (IRM 2002; ERM 2004; Curtis and Carey 2012). The accepted steps of a risk management process, as applied by business organizations, are described below, as well as their application for the risk management process described in this Brief, which was applied for STEM education in Israel. Additional details about the research process are presented in Sect. 3.2.

(1) **Formulation of the strategic objectives of the organization.** In this step, the organizational goals and objectives, as well as the risk management policy suitable for the organizational culture, are decided upon. The organization senior management usually presents this policy to all the employees of the organization.

The adoption of a risk management process for STEM education requires the identification of the goals and objectives that the system wishes to achieve. The following review of relevant documents (Ministry of Education 2011; Ministry of Education, Culture and Sport 1994) summarizes the *objectives* of STEM education in Israel:

- Building human resources in the STEM fields to maintain the position of the high-tech industry in Israel as an important component of the nation's economy.
- Promotion of equal opportunities for all groups in the Israeli society: STEM education should propose each individual a variety and diverse ways for self-fulfillment and excellence.
- Science and technology are considered as part of the general and basic education needed today (and in the future will be required even more), for anyone who wishes to contribute to society (Ministry of Education, Culture and Sport 1994, p. 9).
- Development of 21st century learning skills, such as higher order thinking strategies, deep understanding, teamwork ability, sense of competence, and self-regulation. These skills are currently demanded due to the enormous changes that took place in the past decade in the global economy, job markets, and business environments (Casner-Lotto and Barrington 2006; Duderstadt 2010; Greenhill 2010; Male et al. 2010).

Accordingly, the stated *goals* for STEM education in Israel are defined as follows (Ministry of Education 2012):

- Establishment of an excellence program in STEM education that will increase the number of graduates who complete their high school studies with a diploma which includes an advanced level (5 units[2]) studies of English, Mathematics, and two science subjects (Physics, Chemistry, Biology, and Computer Science). In the technology education, one of these science subjects can be replaced by an engineering subject.
- Within five years, doubling the number of excellent graduates in the above STEM excellence program (the basis year specified in the report is 2010).

(2) **Event identification.** At this stage, the organization identifies external events (opportunities and threats) and internal events (strengths and weaknesses) that may have either positive or negative impacts on the achievement of the

[2]In Israel, the number of units of each subject matter represents the level of learning of the subject in the high school: One (1) represents the lowest level and five (5) represents the highest level.

organizational objectives and goals, as defined in the previous step. A distinction is made between:

- an event with a negative impact (a downside) which represents a risk, and should be treated by a relief program (mitigation);
- an event with a positive impact (upside) which represents an opportunity that the organization management can channel for the achievement of the objectives set in step # 1.

This phase, the risk identification phase, when implemented for STEM education in Israel was carried out by a SWOT analysis. The SWOT analysis identified risks (internal weaknesses and external threats) as well as opportunities (internal strengths and external opportunities) faced by this education system (see Pahse A: Risk Identification, Chap. 4).

(3) **Risk assessment**. Risk assessment is carried out by the examination of the risk probability (likelihood) and their implications (impact). The likelihood represents the probability that an event, which can damage the organization, will occur; the implication represents the potential damage that the event can cause.

For STEM education in Israel, the phase of risk assessment process (of internal weaknesses and external threats) was implemented by a Delphi survey in which practitioners in STEM education—who hold different roles and belong to different sectors—estimated the risk implications (see Chap. 5). Since we also included in this stage the risk prioritization, this phase is referred in this Brief as Phase B: Risk Rating.

(4) **Risk response**. At this stage, the organization decides on actions whose aim is to reduce the intensity of the risk implications, in order to minimize the harm that the risk may cause to the achievement of the organizational objectives. This is done by applying one of the risk response strategies, including:

- **Avoid**: remove the risk;
- **Mitigate**: reduce the risk likelihood and/or its impact;
- **Transfer**: transfer the loss that a negative event may cause to a third party, such as an insurance company;
- **Share**: share the risk implications with a third party;
- **Accept**: accept the risk implications and do not take any action to lower the probability of the risk likelihood and its impact.

In addition, in this step, organizations also consider strategies by which opportunities will be addressed, including:

- **Exploit**: search for ways how to realize the opportunities;
- **Enhance**: examine how to increase the effect of opportunity;
- **Sharing**: transfer part of (or all) the treatment of the opportunity to another party;

- **Accept**: accept the uncertainty of the opportunity and do not take any proactive actions to exhaust its potential.

As can be seen, overlap exists between the strategies for addressing risks and for addressing opportunities, which can be combined if needed.

In the case described in this Brief, Phase C: Risk Response for STEM education in Israel examined how to approach the risks, as well as the opportunities, by one of the above strategies (see Chap. 6).

(5) **Control Activities**. In this stage, procedures and control activities are established to ensure that the response plan determined by the organization is followed properly.
(6) **Information and Communication**. The target of this stage is to ensure the ability to identify and collect relevant information at any time in order to enable the various parties of the organization to perform their jobs successfully. It is important to ensure information flow in all directions in the organization: top-down, bottom-up, and across organizational levels.
(7) **Monitoring**. This stage ensures that the risk management process continues smoothly over time, including (a) continuous assessment of the risks that have already been identified and are treated continuously, and at the same time, (b) the identification of new risks as well as how they should be treated by one of the above mentioned strategies.

As can be seen, risk management is a repeated, ongoing process of identification-assessment-response, applied both for risks that have already been identified in the past as well as for new risks which are identified by the organization during this process.

2.5 Summary

One of the key documents in the field of risk management is ISO 31000 Risk Management (ISO Guide73 2009) which describes the principles and guidelines of the risk management process. According to this document, the process can be used for any organization, regardless of size or sector in which the risk management process is implemented.

The literature review conducted for the purpose of our study showed that risk management is not implemented commonly in the field of education. Muehlbach (2008), who describes the application of a risk management process in continuing education and training, claims that leaders of educational institutions do not understand yet the need for risk management in education. Clearly, in order to prepare the graduates of the education system towards the unknown future, a risk management perspective is needed in education in general and mainly, in STEM education in particular.

This Brief illustrates this approach. In the next four chapters, we describe our examined educational field, that is, STEM education in Israel (Chap. 3), laying out the three stages of risk management applied in our study—risk identification (Chap. 4), risk rating (Chap. 5), and risk response (Chap. 6). We hope that this description illustrates the suitability of risk management processes also for education organizations.

References

Barney, J. (1995). Looking inside for competitive advantage. *The Academy of Management Executive, 4*, 49–61.

Butts, D., Capie, W., Fuller, E., May, D., Okey, J., & Yeany, R. (1978). Priorities for research in science education: a Delphi study. *Journal of Research in Science Teaching, 15*(2), 109–114.

Bruckner, R. M., List, B., & Schiefer, J. (2001). Developing requirements for data warehouse systems with use cases, In Proceedings of the *Seventh Americas Conference on Information Systems* (AMCIS 2001), Boston, Massachusetts, USA, 329–335.

Casner-Lotto, J., & Barrington, L. (2006). Are *They Really Ready to Work? Employers' Perspectives on the Basic Knowledge and Applied Skills of New Entrants to the 21st Century US Workforce*. Partnership for 21st Century Skills.

Curtis, P., & Carey, M., (2012). Risk Assessment in Practice-Research Commissioned by COSO.

Duderstadt, J. J. (2010). Engineering for a changing world: A roadmap to the future of American engineering practice, research, and education, in D. Grasso and M. B. Burkins (eds). *Holistic Engineering Education: Beyond Technology*. New York: Springer, pp. 17–39.

ERM, (2004). *Enterprise Risk Management —Integrated Framework: Executive summery*. The Committee of Sponsoring Organizations of the Treadway Commission. http://www.coso.org/documents/coso_erm_executivesummary.pdf

Godet, M. (2008). *Strategic Foresight La Prospective*. Paris: Dunod.

Greenhill, V. (2010). *21st Century Knowledge and Skills in Educator Preparation*. Partnership for 21st Century Skills.

Helmer, O. (1966). *Social Technology*. Basic Books, New York.

Hussler, C., Muller, P., & Rondé, P. (2011). Is diversity in Delphi panelist groups useful? Evidence from a French forecasting exercise on the future of nuclear energy. *Technological Forecasting and Social Change, 78*(9), 1642–1653. http://www.risk-doctor.com/docs/Hillson%20Opportunity%20responses%20PMI%20Nov01.pdf

Hasson, F., & Keeney, S. (2011). Enhancing rigour in the Delphi technique research. *Technological Forecasting and Social Change, 78*(9), 1695–1704.

Hosseinzadehdastak, F., & Underdown, P. E. (2012). An analysis of risk management methods. *Proceedings of the IIE Annual Conference*, p. 1. Institute of Industrial Engineers-Publisher.

IRM (2002). *Risk Management Standard*. The Institute of Risk Management (IRM), The Association of Insurance and Risk Managers (AIRMIC) and the National Forum for Risk Management in the Public Sector (ALARM). https://www.theirm.org/media/886059/ARMS_2002_IRM.pdf.

ISO Guide 73. (2009). *Risk management – Vocabulary: a collection of terms and definitions relating to the management of risk*. International Organization for Standardization. http://www.iso.org/iso/home/standards/iso31000.htm

Linstone, H., & Turoff, M. (1975). *The Delphi Method*. Addison-Wesley Publication.

Male, S. A., Bush, M. B., & Chapman, E. S. (2010). Perceptions of competency deficiencies in engineering graduates. *Australasian Journal of Engineering Education*, 16(1), 55.

Mikes, A., & Kaplan, R. S. (2014). *Towards a Contingency Theory of Enterprise Risk Management*. Harvard Business School.

Ministry of Education, Culture and Sport (1994). *Tomorrow 98: Report of the Sperior Committee on Science, Mathematics and Technology Education in Israel*, Publications Department, Ministry of Education, Culture and Sport.

Ministry of Education (2011). Adapting the Education system to the 21st Century Master Document Version 11 31-08-2011, Hebrew full document: http://cms.education.gov.il/NR/rdonlyres/79B5A8CF-F812-4A63-89BE-3BEFEB887EC5/142454/12.pdf, English Summary: http://cms.education.gov.il/EducationCMS/Units/MadaTech/englishsifria/AdaptingtheEducationSystemtothe21Century/Vision_and_rationale.htm

Ministry of Education (2012). Preparing the Future Leadership in Science and Technology, http://cms.education.gov.il/NR/rdonlyres/E0B8F780-137D-4785-969D-208790D983E6/124762/av16022011.pdf

Muehlbach, D. (2008). *Risk Management Content Analysis: Understanding the Relationship with Continuing Education Planning*. A Dissertation for the Degree Doctor of Philosophy. Capella University.

Nakatsu, R. T., & Iacovou, C. L. (2009). A comparative study of important risk factors involved in offshore and domestic outsourcing of software development projects: A two-panel Delphi study. *Information & Management*, *46*(1), 57–68.

Nag, R., Hambrick, D. C., & Chen, M. J. (2007). What is strategic management, really? Inductive derivation of a consensus definition of the field. *Strategic management journal*, *28*(9), 935–955.

Rego, G., & Nunes, R. (2010). Hospital Foundation: A SWOT Analysis. *IBusiness, 2*, 210–217.

Rowe, G., & Wright, G. (2011). The Delphi technique: Past, present, and future prospects—Introduction to the special issue. *Technological Forecasting and Social Change*, *78*(9), 1487–1490.

Sabbaghi, A., & Vaidyanathan, G. (2004). SWOT Analysis and Theory of Constraint in Information Technology Projects. *Information Systems Education, Journal*, *2*(23), 1–19.

Chapter 3
STEM Education in Israel: A Case Study

Abstract In this chapter, we review the STEM education system in Israel, including historical overview, current reforms and contemporary trends and emphasis. We also describe the research process of the risk management process presented in this Brief, including the *Research Methodology* (Sect. 3.2.1), *Research Participants* (Sect. 3.2.2) and *Research Tools* (Sect. 3.2.3), and the *Research Process* (Sect. 3.2.4).

Keywords STEM education · Risk management · Research methodology · Research participants · Research tools · Research process

3.1 STEM Education in Israel: Past and Present

In what follows, the main reforms and changes which characterize STEM education in Israel are described. The description is divided into four periods of time—from the establishment of the state of Israel in 1948 until today. The description is partially based on Vorgan and Nathan (2008).

Period A—the 50s and 60s (20th century): Vocational studies were promoted and about one-fifth of the students were directed to study vocational two-year studies. However, the status of vocational education was low, and it was fostered mainly in the peripheral areas of Israel. At the same time, modern Hebrew education, established in the new state of Israel, emphasized theoretical studies and was considered on a higher level dedicated for the more educated pupils.

At the same time, the Israeli industry developed rapidly, and the demand for workers, mainly, technicians and practical engineers, increased. Consequently, the number of students in vocational schools was increased and at the end of the decade reached to 40% of the high school pupils. The study framework of vocational education was changed from two-years to four-year, additional theoretical studies, such as the Bible and English, were added, in order to train educated professionals. In addition, traditional theoretical high school opened vocational education tracks.

A. Even Zahav and O. Hazzan, *Risk Management of Education Systems*, SpringerBriefs in Education, DOI 10.1007/978-3-319-51984-5_3

Nevertheless, the vocational education tracks during this period were still perceived as tracks which fit mainly for students who failed in other educational frameworks, and was considered as a second choice mainly for pupils with low Israeli socioeconomic background from the peripheral parts of Israel.

As we shall see later in this Brief, this status of vocational education continues influencing the society of Israel in general and its education system in particular for many years. Only today, with the introduction of new updated courses into vocational education, its status starts changing and it is found attractive for many high school pupils from different academic levels, sectors, socioeconomic backgrounds, and geographical areas of Israel.

Period B—the 70s and 80s (20th century): Until the late 70s, the percentage of students studying vocational education has increased and reached 52%—the highest level ever in Israel. Then, this percentage has been stabilized for about two decades, and in the late 80s, started declining dramatically in favor of academic theoretical-oriented education.

In the early 70s, structural changes were introduced into the education system. Among them, comprehensive schools were established with two main education paths:

- Academic-oriented theoretical path which lead to high school diploma (with a full matriculation examination diploma) eligible for academic studies;
- Technology education path that includes three tracks of study, each of them has its curriculum and examination system, *without providing students mobility between the different tracks*.
  - Practical professional studies—for students with the lowest achievements;
  - Regular professional studies—for students with medium achievements;
  - High professional studies—for students with high achievements that allow them to get a matriculation diploma eligible for academic studies.

Not surprising, this change raised criticism, not only from social organizations who claimed for inequity, but also from the industry, which claimed that the vocational education system does not provide the students with the needed skills and updated knowledge required for the industry.

Period C—the 90s (20th century): During this period, vocational education continued declining, while in parallel, the number of students who chose to study in the academic-oriented theoretical path increased.

In November 1990, the Minister of Education appointed a committee to examine the level and scope of science and technology education in Israel. The committee included representatives from the academia, the military, the industry, and the education system. In August 1992, the final report was submitted: *Tomorrow 98': Report of the Superior Committee on Science, Mathematics, and Technology Education in Israel* (Ministry of Education, Culture and Sport 1994). The committee's main recommendations were:

- to expand the scientific basis of the students in the technology education tracks, and to update the curricula accordingly;
- to reduce the number of courses in the technology education path (so that the differences between the courses be significant);
- to reduce the number of hours of practical training, by postponing the selection of this study track to the eleventh grade, when the pupils are more mature.

As a result of these recommendations, the curriculum was updated, the option to complete high school with a diploma of 12 years of studying was eliminated, and the option to take the matriculation exam (and to finish high school with a matriculation diploma) was offered to all the students in all tracks.

Period D—the 2000s: During these years, Israel's industry has been based more and more on science and engineering and started being influenced more and more by globalization processes. These processes required strengthening and developing world-class human capital and worker mobility between different sectors and domains. These trends naturally led to an increase in the number of students who choose the technology education tracks, and in parallel, the need for high-quality STEM teachers increased.

As can be seen, the focus of the different kinds of education has been changed during these years, especially the importance attributed to technology and STEM education. As we shall see later in this Brief, these changed continued influencing Israel's education system for many years, constituting some of the risks with which STEM education in Israel faces today.

3.2 Research Framework

This section describes the research framework of the risk management process presented in this Brief. We describe the research methodology (Sect. 3.2.1), the research participants (Sect. 3.2.2) the research tools (Sect. 3.2.3), and the research process (Sect. 3.2.4).

3.2.1 Research Methodology

The research method was mixed and used both qualitative (the main one) and quantitative research tools. The qualitative method allowed describing the perspective of the study participants and was used to analyze the data gathered by the Delphi survey.

3.2.2 Research Participants

The research participants participated in the three phases of the study (several of them participated in the three phases): Phase A: Risk identification; Phase B: Risk rating; and Phase C: Risk response. They belonged to the following two groups.

Group I: Employees of the education system—total of 117[1]

- STEM Teachers who teach in the secondary school the following subjects: Mathematics, Physics, Chemistry, Biology, Computer science, and the Technology education subjects. They all have a teaching certificate, at least a Master's degree, and a teaching experience of at least five years. They all prepare their students toward the matriculation exams in all levels.
- High school principals.
- Administrative executive role holders in the education system, local councils, and school chains.

These participants had a direct contact with the education system. They all work in the field of STEM education in Israel and face challenges while performing their role in the system.

These research participants were interviewed in an in-depth interviews designed as a SWOT analysis (Phase A of the study—the risk identification phase), in which they were asked to describe each of the SWOT analysis component with respect to STEM education in Israel, on the individual, the school, the STEM education curriculum, and the national levels. At the following phases, the risk rating (Phase B) and risk response (Phase C), additional data were collected from this group by the SWOT interview, questionnaires, and focus groups.

Group II: Managerial role holders in organizations involved in STEM education—total of 167[2]

These research participants belong to four groups of stakeholders: academia, industry, military, and nonprofit NGOs. Data were collected from this group at an advanced stage of Phase A of the study, in Phase B by questionnaires, and in Phase C by focus groups. This group represented a wide range of expertise from various fields and, thus, provided a broad and diverse perspective on STEM education in Israel. In our research, they contributed to the building of a strategic plan that copes with current and future challenges of STEM education in Israel. We selected stakeholders who are familiar with STEM education, serve in key roles, and cooperate with the education system in order to promote STEM education. The criteria guided the selection of these participants were:

---

[1]Since several participants participated in more than one phase of the study, some overlap may exist.

[2]Since several participants participated in more than one phase of the study, some overlap may exist.

- Hold an academic background in one of the following disciplines: science and engineering, education, management, and education policy.
- Hold either a current or a previous position with an interface to STEM education.
- Have an experience in organizational strategic planning.
- Hold a decision making position in their organization.
- Are acquainted with the challenges of STEM education in Israel and in other countries.

3.2.3 Research Tools

Data was collected using the following research tools: interviews, questionnaires, focus groups, documents, and researcher log.

SWOT Interview

The SWOT interview was designed as a semi-structured, in-depth interview in order to reveal the perception of the research participants with respect to STEM education in Israel.

The interview was built according to the four components of the SWOT analysis and was adapted to each group of the research participants. The analysis of the interviews showed that this framework allowed the interviewees to elaborate beyond the focus of the question and to express their perspective on additional related issues.

Questionnaires

Questionnaires were designed mainly as a Delphi survey to collect data in the process of risk rating (Phase B) and in the formulation of the response plan (Phase C).

Based on the data analysis carried out in Phase A, a "Risk management—Risk rating" questionnaire was designed in Phase B. The purpose of the questionnaire was to validate the data analysis of Phase A, as well as to assess and prioritize the risks, and their implications for STEM education in Israel.

The questionnaire asked the research participants to rate the risks on a Likert scale. The data was analyzed by descriptive statistics (mean, standard deviation, etc.) and statistical tests. One factor F-test was used to examine differences between the risk ratings of the five groups of stakeholders.

At the same time, the open questions included in the questionnaire were analyzed qualitatively. This analysis added data to our study and validated the findings of the previous phases.

In addition, we designed questionnaires for specific purposes. For example, we distributed a questionnaire to the schools participated in the study whose aim was to check the conjecture according to which STEM teachers rarely serve in leadership roles at school (that turned out to be true in the schools participated in the study).

Focus Groups

Focus group were used in Phase C—risk response plan. Focus groups emphasize the interaction between group members depending on the issues brought to them, when the researcher plays as a mediator.

We facilitated nine focus groups in which fifty practitioners, from the two groups of the research population described above, participated. Each focus group included representatives from the five groups of stakeholders—education, academia, industry, military, and nonprofit NGOs. In addition to reaching a consensus related to the risk prioritization, the participants examined strategies to mitigate the identified risks.

Documents

Documents were analyzed to further validate our findings by formal publications, such as, regulations published periodically by the Ministry of Education, committee reports, school websites, principal messages to teachers, etc.

3.2.4 Research Process

The study was carried out during four years (2012–2015) in three phases: Risk identification (Phase A), risk rating (Phase B), and response plan (Phase C), as described in what follows.

Phase A—Risk Identification

April 2012–January 2013

- SWOT interview with STEM teachers (Group A) and SWOT analysis of STEM education in Israel as perceived by the STEM teachers
- Document analysis: Committee reports, protocols of meetings, and documents of national programs of the Ministry of Education
- First round of Delphi survey: Risks identification.

January 2013–February 2014

- SWOT interview with school principals (Group A)
- SWOT analysis of STEM education in Israel as perceived by school principals and policy makers in the Ministry of Education (Group A).

March 2014–July 2014

- SWOT interview with stakeholders in STEM education (Group B)
- Documents analysis: Committees reports, protocols of meetings, and documents of national programs of the Ministry of Education

- SWOT analysis of STEM education in Israel as perceived by stakeholders in STEM education
- Construction of the integrated SWOT analysis of STEM education in Israel.

Phase B—Risk Rating, ***August 2014–February 2015***

- Delphi survey: Questionnaire "Risk management—Risk rating." The questionnaire was designed based on the integrated SWOT analysis (Groups A and B). Section 5.1 adds details about the formulation (Sect. 5.1.1), distribution (Sect. 5.1.2), and analysis (Sect. 5.1.3) of the questionnaire.
- Analysis of the "Risk management—Risk rating" questionnaire.

Phase C—Risk Response

March 2015–July 2015

- Delphi survey (continued)
- Focus groups "Risk management—Response plan." These focus groups were dedicated to the formulation of the response plan. As a preparation for these focus groups, a "Risk management—re-rating and response" questionnaire was distributed to the participants one day before the group meets. It includes both parts of the "Risk management—Risk rating" questionnaire (Phase B), to further validate its results, as well as questions that ask to propose courses of action that address the risks whose severity are considered high by the participant.
- SWOT interview with stakeholders
- Document analysis: Summaries of panels and conferences on STEM education, protocols of meetings, and documents of national programs of the Ministry of Education
- Data analysis: Focus groups, questionnaire "Risk management—re-rating, and response," SWOT interviews.

August 2015–December 2015

- A preliminary summary of the risk management process which laid out a risk management program for STEM Education in Israel
- Reanalysis of the data collected in all phases
- Formulation of the framework of the research findings: Proposed strategic risk management program for STEM education in Israel.

3.3 Summary

In this chapter, we presented a historical review of STEM education in Israel and described the research framework used for the risk management process applied for this system. These descriptions set the stage for the detailed description of the three phases of the risk management process (described in Chaps. 4, 5 and 6) we implemented for STEM education in Israel.

References

Ministry of Education, Culture and Sport (1994). *Tomorrow 98: Report of the Superior Committee on Science, Mathematics and Technology Education in Israel*, Publications Department, Ministry of Education, Culture and Sport.

Vorgan, Y. and Nathan, G. (2008). *Vocational and Technological Education in Israel and the World*, The Knesset Center for Research and Information, Jerusalem (Hebrew). https://www.knesset.gov.il/mmm/data/pdf/m02141.pdf.

Chapter 4
Phase A: Risk Identification—Identification of Risk Categories by SWOT Analysis of STEM Education in Israel

Abstract This chapter describes the risk identification by SWOT analysis of STEM education in Israel. It outlines seven risk categories of 43 risk factors, based on bureaucratic-professional conflicts and barriers in implementing changes in education systems.

Keywords Risk management · STEM education · Risk identification · SWOT analysis · Risk categories · Risk factors · Bureaucratic-professional conflicts · Barriers in implementing changes in education systems

4.1 Conflicts and Barriers

The SWOT analysis of STEM Education in Israel led to identification of two perceptions of the study participants with respect to how they conceive the weaknesses and threats of STEM Education. The STEM teachers' perception, the professional educators, who perceive themselves as educational agents (Hativa 2008), present *conflicts* they face with the system. All other stakeholders of STEM education present *barriers* they face when coping with changes they wish to introduce to STEM education. While the STEM teachers' perception reflects a personal and professional introspective of the nature of STEM education, the stakeholders' viewpoint reflects a broad perspective of STEM education.

4.1.1 The Bureaucratic-Professional Conflict

The perspective of the STEM teachers reflects the *bureaucratic-professional conflict* that causes them difficulties in realizing their professional goals (Hall 1967). As a result, the organization, namely, the STEM education system, is unable to achieve its goals. In particular, STEM teachers face five conflicts whose essence is the teachers as professionals versus the system in which they work: (a) the professional

A. Even Zahav and O. Hazzan, *Risk Management of Education Systems*,
SpringerBriefs in Education, DOI 10.1007/978-3-319-51984-5_4

opportunities conflict, (b) the teacher status conflict, (c) the academic freedom conflict, (d) the profession perception conflict, and (e) the discourse on STEM education conflict.

- **The professional opportunities conflict** deals with the limited professional opportunities, professional development, and career promotion tracks available for the STEM teachers. STEM teachers are in conflict with the education system which, according to their perception, does not create opportunities for their professional development that lies primarily in the limited administrative track (Barak 2011). It is apparent that STEM teachers are more interested in the development of the professional aspects of their careers, and less in the administrative aspects. In particular, the STEM teachers who participated in the study expressed the desire to fill research and development (R&D) positions, in which they would engage in curriculum development, serve as the teachers of teachers, study toward their PhDs, and fulfill leadership roles in the education system.
- **The teacher status conflict** is expressed in the salary level, the social benefits and pension, and the working environment, e.g., poor laboratory equipment and lack of sitting spaces. The conflict is between the teachers' self-perception as professional STEM teachers—people who have been trained for their jobs in academic institutions, hold academic degrees in the subjects they teach, and wish to pursue their professional development—and the way in which the system perceives them (and to a large extent, the society as a whole).
- **The academic freedom conflict** refers to the professional teachers' need for academic freedom, i.e., their demand for professional autonomy, which reflects a central characteristic of professionalism (Hall 1968). In general, the more rigid the system is and the more stringent rules it dictates, the less academic freedom is provided for the professionals. Specifically, the STEM teachers mentioned that academic freedom is denied from them in many ways, such as, choosing the study contents and level, determining the allocation of teaching hours to the subject they teach, and participating in decision-making processes related to the level and structure of the matriculation exam.
- **The profession perception conflict** embodies the clash between the STEM teachers' perception of how science subjects should be taught and that of the organization. Such a confrontation is created when the organization operates in a way that contradicts the characteristics of the teachers' professionalism: their social commitment, their devotion to the profession, their belief in self-supervision, and their demand for professional autonomy (Hall 1968). The STEM teachers' perceptions relate to aspects such as, how to teach STEM subjects to students with different abilities and the teaching—content and teaching methods—of science and technology subjects at the junior high school. The teachers are compelled to obey the organization's requirements and when these requirements contradict their views, the said conflict arises.
- **The discourse on STEM education conflict** expresses the STEM teachers' high level of professional devotion and social commitment (Hall 1968). In their opinion, the way in which the organization operates contradicts (a) their social

commitment as professional teachers who encourage their students to enter the world of science learning and (b) the importance they attribute to the need of the society for a growing number of scientists and engineers. Thus, according to the teachers' understanding, when the education system does not project the importance of STEM education to school principals and through them to the students, the number of students who choose to study science declines, and their conflict with the organization exacerbates. Teachers noted that the school board usually determines the discourse about the importance of the STEM subjects based on the professional background of the school management, which in the schools participated in our study, was mainly social and liberal arts (and not one of the STEM subjects). In addition, teachers noted that the school assessment method in Israel, which is determined according to a school's matriculation exam eligibility and scores, and not by the subjects the students learn, contradicts their efforts to promote the learning of STEM subjects.

The bureaucratic-professional conflict explains some of the shortage of professional STEM teachers currently experienced in Israel as well as the expected future shortages of qualified STEM teachers. These shortages pose a risk for the STEM education system and, accordingly, methods for coping with this risk are presented as part of the risk response phase (Sect. 6.3.1).

4.1.2 Barriers in Change Processes

The perspective of the other stakeholders of STEM education in Israel presented barriers to STEM education (Havelock and Huberman 1977) which introduce difficulties to implement changes in the system. In particular, the stakeholders' perceptions reflected the following five barriers: (a) economic barrier, (b) procedural barrier, (c) psychological-personal barrier, (d) sociocultural barrier, and (e) political barrier.

- **The economic barrier** stems from the limited budget allocated for STEM education reforms. The economic barrier is expressed in difficulties implementing STEM project, the budget provided for schools to open technology education tracks and operate technology classes, and the budget allocated for the renewal of science and technology laboratories.
- **The procedural barrier** reflects the difficulties to lead changes in the education system, such as deficiencies in recruiting new teachers when lack of procedural process for guidance and absorption of new teachers leads to loss of teachers in the early years in their jobs, lack of training program to in-service teachers when adopting new national reform program, and lack of science education of teachers who teach science in the elementary school. Sometimes, this barrier arises as a result of lack of coordination between those involved in the implementation of change processes in the education system; sometimes, it is expressed in outsourcing of educational programs, meaning, entrance of external

bodies from the business sector, and other NGOs to the STEM education system. The outsourcing process of education is challenging, since on the one hand, these bodies promote their interests and needs, and on the other hands, the system desires to promote STEM education and to increase the number of students participating in STEM programs. For example, in STEM programs for female students, the identity of the curriculum director was unclear: Is it the Division of Science and Technology of the Ministry of Education or is it the body who, in practice, implements the program?

- **The psychological-personal barrier** reflects the psychological barrier of some groups in the Israeli society to be part of the transformation processes that take place in the education system. It is expressed, for example, in the gender gap in the participation of female and male students in STEM education, and students' self-perceptions about their abilities to succeed in scientific professions.
- **The sociocultural barrier** refers to cultural differences in the values and beliefs among different groups in Israel. In the context of STEM education, it is expressed, for example, in barriers to introduce changes in the ultraorthodox education system, such as, the enforcement of STEM studies. It is also expressed in social perceptions that link vocational education to groups belonging to low socioeconomic level.
- **The political barrier** stems due to the rapid turnover of governments and key figures in the public service, each of them pursuing a different agenda. A comprehensive educational reform needs strong political leadership that enjoys public support and strains future planning and the development of learning organization culture (Argyris and Schon 1978) in STEM education. Chen (2005) notes that this culture development requires a change that is planned and controlled, in which the system relies on the organizational memory, analyzes past processes of long-term scale, and allows to implement "Lessons learned" processes and future design. Stakeholders addressed the need for future planning, together with the establishment of a measurement and control system for the implementation of long-term programs. However, the government frequent turnover and the political need for immediate results usually prevent long-term planning.

4.2 Seven Risk Categories

The above conflicts and barriers represent the study participants' perceptions of external threats and internal weaknesses of STEM education in Israel. In what follows, these threats and weaknesses are referred as "risk factors."

Forty-three risk factors were identified and grouped into seven risk categories: (a) Sectors in STEM education, (b) Teacher—opportunities, training and social status, (c) Curriculum of STEM subjects; (d) Study sequences—school, higher education, military, labor market, (e) Management of STEM education, (f) Social perceptions, and (g) National programs in STEM education. Table 4.1 lists the 43 risk factors by the seven risk categories.[1] Table 4.1 also presents the conflicts and barriers each risk factor belongs to.

Table 4.2, is derived from Table 4.1, summarizing the links between the categories, conflicts, and barriers. As can be seen, the only two categories addressed both by the STEM teachers and the other stakeholders are (2) Teachers—opportunities, training and social status and (5) Management of STEM education. This observation further amplifies the importance attributed to the role of STEM teachers in Israel.

The following sections review the seven risk categories according to the risk factors each of them represents.

4.2.1 Risk Category: Sectors in STEM Education

This category refers to the diminished representation in STEM education of certain sectors of the Israeli society: students from the Israeli economic and social periphery, the ultraorthodox sector, female students, and the Arab sector. The roots of the diminished representation of these sectors in STEM education are social and cultural characteristics and historical processes.

- **Ultraorthodox sector**: Cultural and procedural characteristics led to the current situation—ultraorthodox schools for males do not teach STEM studies.
  The Israeli Ministry of Education is divided into four different subsystems, one for each community that differs in its national identity, religion, and language. One of these subsystems is the ultraorthodox branch of education, whose schools are unofficial independent schools and is characterized by a scholastic content variability (Dovrat 2005). The expression of this process is that most of the core studies[2] are not taught in the ultraorthodox schools for males.
- **The Arab sector and students associated with the Israeli socioeconomic periphery**: The limited representation of these two groups in the study of advanced level science subjects reflects a historical process which is publicly criticized by the Israeli society. These two sectors were tracked to vocational education during the early years of the establishment of the state of Israel. The research participants expressed the threat of renewing this past "stain" of vocational education: Directing students from the Israeli periphery to low-tech technology education tracks (technology and occupational tracks. See terminology), which limit both their educational and professional opportunities.

[1]In fact, at the end of the Identification Phase, 61 risk factors were elicited. After a validation process, the 43 risk factors, presented in Table 4.1, were found to be meaningful. See also Sect. 5.1.1.

[2]The following subjects are considered core studies in Israel: Mathematics, English, religious studies (each sector studies its religion), Literature, Chemistry, Physics, Biology, and History.

Table 4.1 Risk categories, conflicts, and barriers: the 43 risk factors of STEM education in Israel

Risk categories	Conflicts	Barriers	Risk factors
1. Sectors in STEM education		Psychological-personal barrier Sociocultural barrier Procedural barrier	1. Most of the ultraorthodox female students do not study science courses on the advanced level in high school*
			2. Male students in ultraorthodox schools do not study STEM subjects at all*
			3. Many students attending military[a] classes are associated with social-economic periphery
			4. Many students attending vocational education are associated with social-economic periphery
			5. Percentage of students studying advanced level science subjects among male students is higher than among female students*
			6. If a female student faces difficulty in learning advanced science subject, there is a tendency to suggest her to study the subject on a lower level*
2. Teachers—opportunities, training and social status	Professional opportunities conflict Teacher status conflict	Procedural barrier	7. Lack of promotion tracks for STEM teachers*
			8. The teaching profession is not appreciated by the public*
			9. STEM teachers' salary is low relative to alternatives jobs in the industry*
			10. The working conditions of STEM teachers are not attractive*
			11. Placement and guidance of novice STEM teachers is not provided
			12. Many teachers who teach science in elementary school lack education in the field
			13. Only small number of junior high school teachers who teach "Science and Technology" are Physics or Chemistry teachers
			14. Number of students who study STEM education in universities is low

(continued)

Table 4.1 (continued)

Risk categories	Conflicts	Barriers	Risk factors
			15. Lack of a collaborative professional community for STEM teachers
3. Curriculum of STEM subjects	Profession perception conflict		16. Technological aspects are not sufficiently integrated in science studies in the elementary school
			17. Structure and content of STEM education in junior high schools: The subject "Science and Technology" is taught as one block of four disciplines (Biology, Chemistry, Physics and technology)*
			18. Frequent changes in the curricula of STEM subjects
			19. The curriculum of the vocational education subjects does not match the needs of the labor market*
			20. The teaching of STEM subjects focuses mainly on the preparation toward the matriculation exams
4. Study sequences—school, higher education, military, labor market		Procedural barrier	21. Long training is needed to prepare high school graduates for technological jobs in the military service
			22. Shortage of engineers in the industry*
			23. Shortage of practical engineers and technicians in the industry*
			24. Shortage of skilled low-tech professionals in the industry
			25. Lack of career plan programs for high school students
			26. Universities are required to offer preparatory courses for high school graduates before accepting them to undergraduate science and engineering studies to close gaps in the STEM subjects
5. Management of STEM education	Academic freedom conflict Discourse on STEM education conflict	Procedural barrier Economic barrier	27. Tight supervision over teachers and principals*
			28. Bureaucratic work is required from principals and teachers
			29. School success is measured by the eligibility of a matriculation certificate and not by the subjects included in the certificate

(continued)

Table 4.1 (continued)

Risk categories	Conflicts	Barriers	Risk factors
			30. Lax discipline in schools
			31. Parents' involvement in schools*
			32. Involvement of military and industry in STEM education in the high school*
			33. Limited budget to open technology classes
6. Social perceptions		Psychological-personal barrier Sociocultural barrier	34. Negative labeling of vocational education*
			35. Vocational jobs are not valued*
			36. The perception "I am not qualified for studying science subjects" is common among students*
			37. The perception "It is better to study easier subjects" is common among students*
			38. The perception "Vocational education is associated with social gaps in the Israeli society" is common in the public*
7. National programs in STEM education		Procedural barrier Political barrier	39. The introduction of new national programs reduces the importance attributed to previous national programs
			40. Lack of teacher training process prior the implementation of a new national program*
			41. Lack of persistence in the implementation of long-term national programs*
			42. Budgets for infrastructure, teaching and training hours are increased especially when a crisis is identified
			43. Implementation of national programs without appropriate infrastructure*

The reviewed risk factors are denoted by *
[a]The students in these classes learn professions required by the army

Table 4.2 Risk categories, conflicts and barriers

Risk categories	Conflicts	Barriers
1. Sectors in STEM education		Psychological-personal barrier Sociocultural barrier Procedural barrier
2. Teachers—opportunities, training, and social status	Professional opportunities conflict Teacher status conflict	Procedural barrier
3. Curriculum of STEM subjects	Profession perception conflict	
4. Study sequences—school, higher education, military, labor market		Procedural barrier
5. Management of STEM education	Academic freedom conflict Discourse on STEM education conflict	Procedural barrier Economic barrier
6. Social perceptions		Psychological-personal barrier Sociocultural barrier
7. National programs in STEM education		Procedural barrier Political barrier

Attempts are being made to change this trend today, as is described in Phase C of the study (Sect. 6.3.4).

- **Female students**: The diminished representation of female students in STEM education is well known worldwide, mainly in Western countries. It is usually explained by female students' tendency to choose a theoretical/humanities tracks and is linked to social perceptions that characterize STEM professions as male occupations. Attempts are also made currently in Israel, as in other countries, in this context (Phase C, Sect. 6.4.3).

The risk factors in this category are listed in Table 4.3 and are described below.

Risk factors 1, 5, and 6: Gender gaps in the participation of students in STEM studies

Data from the Israeli Ministry of Education show the relatively low percentages of high school female students who choose to study STEM subjects relative to male students. In particular, a significant gap observed in the following subjects: Physics and Technology education subjects, such as Computer Science and Electronics.

In the school year 2013–2014, the percentages of female students who studied the following subjects at the advanced level were: 45% Mathematics; 36% Physics;

Table 4.3 Sectors in STEM education—barriers and risk factors

Barriers	Risk factors
Psychological-personal barrier Sociocultural barrier Procedural barrier	1. Most of the ultraorthodox female students do not study science subjects on the advanced level in high school*
	2. Male students in ultraorthodox schools do not study STEM subjects at all*
	3. Many students attending military[a] classes are associated with social-economic periphery
	4. Many students attending vocational education are associated with social-economic periphery
	5. Percentage of students studying advanced level science subjects among male students is higher than among female students*
	6. If a female student faces difficulty in learning advanced science subject, there is a tendency to suggest her to study the subject on a lower level*

*The reviewed risk factors are starred
[a]The students in these classes learn different professions as is required by the military

33% Computer Science; and 35% Electronics. The opposite trend observed in the two science subjects Chemistry and Biology. The percentages of female students studying these subjects were 64% for Chemistry and 65% for Biology.[3]

The STEM stakeholders argued that school counselors tend to refer female students to lower level studies of STEM subjects.

A., a senior military personnel, engaged in recruiting students to technology education tracks, described her perspective with respect to how gender gaps are generated:

> The stigma that exists primarily among educational counselors… to refer female students to 'softer' subjects, less technological. There are very few who choose to study Physics, as a result, there are very few female in academic reserve tracks[4]… their attitude 'If it is difficult, attend a class of a lower level, leave the advanced level' is delivered mainly to female students but not only.

A variety of solutions are currently designed to close these gaps. Most of them approach underrepresented groups in the STEM subjects in Israel and deliver the importance of studying in the science and technology courses in the high schools. These courses are marketed as opportunity openers to interesting occupation during

[3]This percentages were compiled by the Szold Institute based on data provided at the *Virtual Research Room* of the Ministry of Education: http://cms.education.gov.il/EducationCMS/Applications/spss/dafault.htm.

[4]An academic reserve track is offered to high school students with excellent scores in the matriculation exams. They can choose this track after graduating from high school and before joining the obligatory service in the IDF (Israeli Defense Force). These students usually work in the army in the discipline they studied in the academia.

one's life, since the skills the students acquire while studying these subjects will serve them in the future job market.

In the *Arab* sector, the percentage of female students who study advanced level STEM subjects is higher than male students. The percentages of female students in the Arab sector, who study Mathematics, Physics, Computer Science, and Electronics at the advanced level, are 60, 57, 53, and 56%, respectively.[5] In the *Jewish* sector, the percentage of female students studies these STEM studies is 42; 29; 30; and 18% respectively. Notably, while in Mathematics, Physics, Computer Science, and Electronics a difference exists in the female students representations between the two sectors, in both sectors the percentage of female students study Chemistry and Biology at the advanced level is higher than the percentage of male students [Data compiled by Szold Institute (See footnote 3)].

The education system refers to this trend as an opportunity to increase the number of students studying science subjects. Mr. Muhanna Fares, the leader of a national program of the Ministry of Education its aim is to promote science and mathematics excellence, refers to a 5 years plan—*Mathematics First* or 5 × 2—to multiply the number of students who study (and complete) the most advanced level of mathematics in high school[6]:

> I intend to achieve the goal of the program by exploiting the potential of all sectors as well as exploiting the potential of female students. We will work in the Arab [sector], Bedouin [sector], Ethiopian [in the Jews sector], to reduce the gaps between female and males who [graduate with a] matriculation exams. With a wise investment in these students, we can transfer them to an advanced level of studies [in math and science]… If we close these gaps in the number of students graduating with advanced level [mathematics and sciences], it will be possible to achieve half of the goals of the program ["Mathematics First"] easily.

Risk factor 2: Male students in ultraorthodox schools do not study STEM subjects at all

Data from the Ministry of Education from 2013 indicate an extremely low participation in the study of science subjects in the ultraorthodox sector, especially by male students. We note that in the ultraorthodox sector, female and male students study in separate schools from early stages.

A director of an ultraorthodox school for female students justifies the current situation. He explains that the structure and contents of the studies in the ultraorthodox schools enable students to bridge the gaps in STEM studies and core studies at a later stage in life and to study an academic degree. In the following quote, he emphasizes that the consequences of how STEM subjects are taught in ultraorthodox schools for males:

---

[5]These percentages are calculated out of the total number of students who study these subjects on this level in the sector.

[6]Muhanna Fares: The five math units revolution will arrive also to the Arab sector. *The Marker*, October 10, 2015: http://www.themarker.com/news/1.2743610.

> Two years ago, I started to study for a degree in education. How do you learn and get along with academic studies? It is important to say that people who study the Torah really get great skills… I could study engineering maybe with more courses to [close the gaps and] meet the qualification … Does Yeshiva [Jewish institution that focuses on the study of traditional religious texts] prepare to be educators? Yes. They do not prepare to work in the high tech, but appropriate plan can bridge the gaps, because the learning skills exist… Physics studies are difficult but possible. A Yeshiva student will succeed where logic and thinking skills are required.

Alongside this position, we are facing currently integration processes of graduates of the ultraorthodox education in the labor market, while training them for positions in the industry. For example, KamaTech[7] is a coalition of 30 leading high-tech companies, innovative startups, and venture funds, which offers training programs for ultraorthodox males. The enterprise was founded as a result of shortage in entrepreneurs and engineers and is also engaged in placing the ultraorthodox sector in jobs, vocational training and allocation of financial grants to ultraorthodox entrepreneurs. The ultimate purpose is to reduce the gap in the representation of this sector in the labor market.

4.2.2 Risk Category: Teachers—Opportunities, Training, and Social Status

This category is presented from two perspectives: the perspective of the STEM teachers and the viewpoint of the other stakeholders of STEM education. The risk factors in this category are listed in Table 4.4 and are described below.

Risk factor 7: Lack of promotion tracks for STEM teachers

As mentioned above, promotion and advancement tracks for STEM teachers, as for all other teachers, lie primarily in the administrative track; therefore, the STEM teachers face a professional-opportunity conflict with the education system, which, they believe, fails to provide them with adequate opportunities for advancing their *teaching* careers. Specifically, the STEM teachers are mostly interested in the development of the professional aspects of their careers, rather than in the promotion of the administrative aspects of their position. In particular, the STEM teachers expressed the desire to fill R&D positions, in which they would engage in the development of learning and teaching curricula, serve as the teachers of teachers, study toward their PhDs, and fulfill leadership roles within the education system.

The STEM teachers referred to this particular weakness of the system, emphasizing the importance they attribute to academic studies in the STEM subjects and

[7]KamaTech website: https://www.kamatech.org.il/english/.

to the need to belong to a broader *professional* community. For example, A., a Physics teacher said:

> The professional development horizon for teachers is very limited… [it is] a critical point: The professional horizon. There's a difference between a Math, Physics or Chemistry teacher and the other teachers, no offence intended… [but] those Math and Physics teachers are a kind of people who don't go into management roles… **a different way must be found. Things like Hemda,**[8] **doing some research, experiments**.

The teachers' words, as expressed in the interviews, raised the question of whether or not STEM teachers only rarely hold administrative positions. We found a partial answer to this question by an online questionnaire distributed to the schools whose teachers participated in the study. It was found that only a small percentage of STEM teachers fill educational and administrative positions. Specifically, on average, 28% of all teachers in the school are STEM teachers, but only 19% of all administrative role-holders in the school are STEM teachers. It is important to mention that even if teachers wish to promote their career in the administrative path, the number of such roles is limited (Barak 2011).

Risk factors 8, 9, and 10: The teaching profession is not appreciated by the public, STEM teachers' salary is low relative to alternatives jobs in the industry, and the working conditions of STEM teachers are not attractive

The teacher status in the public conflicts their own self-perception as professional practitioners who have been trained for their jobs in academic institutions, hold academic degrees in the subjects they teach, and wish to continue their professional development. According to the STEM teachers who participated in the study, teachers' employment conditions (their salary and work environment) reflect the way they are perceived by the system. The STEM teachers mentioned the salary and pension as personal threats that jeopardize the chances they will continue working as teachers.

I., a math teacher, who studied in a second-career program for academic high-tech employees, describes the situation:

> The main threat is the financial issue… If my financial situation is such that I cannot afford it, then I will simply not be able to afford it. I really don't know whether the "Courage for Change" [in Hebrew, Oz Latmura—a reform whose target is to increase teacher salary and status] will make the difference. Thanks to the career-change program in which I participated, I receive a very considerable subsidy on a quarterly basis, … and I still subsidize the education system on a monthly basis.

[8]Hemda is a Science Education Center located in Tel Aviv. Students from schools in the Tel Aviv-Jaffa area come to this center to study Physics, Chemistry, and Computer science. Most of the teachers in Hemda hold a Ph.D. in Physics or Chemistry. The work environment is modern and includes laboratories, computer equipment and demonstration equipment that enable hands-on experience for each and every student. For more details, see Hemda website: http://www.hemda.org.il/english/.

Table 4.4 Teachers—conflicts, barriers, and risk factors

Conflicts	Barriers	Risk factors
Professional opportunities conflict Teacher status conflict	Procedural barrier	7. Lack of promotion tracks for STEM teachers*
		8. The teaching profession is not appreciated by the public*
		9. STEM teachers' salary is low relative to alternatives jobs in the industry*
		10. The working conditions of STEM teachers are not attractive*
		11. Placement and guidance of novice STEM teachers is not provided
		12. Many teachers who teach science in elementary school lack education in the field
		13. Only small number of junior high school teachers who teach "Science and Technology" are Physics or Chemistry teachers
		14. Number of students who study STEM education in universities is low
		15. Lack of a collaborative professional community for STEM teachers

*The reviewed risk factors are starred

4.2.3 Risk Category: Curriculum of STEM Subjects

The risk factors included in this category present the STEM teachers' perspective, related to weaknesses (in the broad sense) of the curriculum of the STEM subjects (that is, not in the context of a specific curriculum of a specific subject). In more details, the STEM teachers' perception reflect aspects such as the desirable number of teaching hours allocated for the STEM subject, the content to be taught, the appropriate teaching methods, and student commitment to study the STEM subjects.

In this case, the profession perception conflict is expressed in a clash between the STEM teacher's perception of how science subjects should be taught and that of the organization. Such a confrontation is created when the organization operates in a way that contradicts the characteristics of the teacher's conception of professionalism: Their social commitment, their devotion to their profession, their belief in self-supervision, and their demand for professional autonomy (Hall 1968). The conflicts and the related risk factors are listed in Table 4.5.

Risk factor 17: Structure and content of STEM education in junior high schools: The subject "Science and Technology" is taught as one block of four disciplines (Biology, Chemistry, Physics, and technology)

Table 4.5 Curriculum—risk factors and the profession perception conflict

Conflicts	Risk factors
Profession perception conflict	16. Technological aspects are not sufficiently integrated in science studies in the elementary school
	17. Structure and content of STEM education in junior high schools: The subject "Science and Technology" is taught as one block of four disciplines (Biology, Chemistry, Physics, and technology)*
	18. Frequent changes in the curricula of STEM subjects
	19. The curriculum of the vocational education subjects does not match the needs of the labor market*
	20. The teaching of STEM subjects focuses mainly on the preparation toward the matriculation exams

*The reviewed risk factors are starred

The high school STEM teachers criticized the way in which STEM education is perceived and implemented in the junior high schools. The teachers pointed out two weaknesses in this context. The first is the curricular level: they believe that the different science subjects should be taught separately as distinct subjects, and not as a single, unified "sciences" subject that includes Physics, Chemistry, Biology, and technology. The second weakness, partially derived from the first one, relates to pedagogical mistakes made in the teaching of this unified subject in the junior high school. These mistakes stem from the fact that the teachers in the junior high school are experts in only one area of (such as Physics or Biology) whereas they are required to teach the entire range of science subjects.

M., a Physics teacher, attested:

> One of the main problems is that Physics is not taught in junior high school… I just screened students for science and technology education tracks. I spoke to ninth grade students and it's just awful. They study what is called "sciences", which they say is like Physics. Actually, it is a mixture of Physics and Biology. It's like having a Biology teacher who is afraid to teach Physics.

The teachers therefore face a conflict. On the one hand, are the professional characteristics, such as their social commitment and devotion to the profession (Hall 1968), while on the other hand, is the dictate of the education system to teach the science subjects as one subject. According to the STEM teachers, the way in which the teaching of science in junior high schools is structured, constitutes a threat to STEM education in general. They expressed their concern that students reach high school with only meager and inaccurate knowledge of science subjects and, as a result, may not choose to study them as part of their matriculation exams on the advanced level.

Thus, K., a Chemistry teacher, said:

> They come with lack of knowledge… They study like parrots, and do not perform enough experiments. It makes me very sad.

Risk factor 19: The curriculum of the vocational education subjects does not match the needs of the labor market

The STEM teachers express the importance they attribute to updated curricula which ensure the students prospects for professional career in the STEM subjects and open options for tertiary education.

The teachers of the vocational subjects expressed the gap between what is being learned in school and what is required in the labor market. They expressed their dedication to the success of the students and the importance they see in an ongoing update process of the curricula and their compliance to the workforce.

This perspective was also highlighted by the other stakeholders, especially in the industry and in the defense system. These stakeholders call the education system to change fundamentally its perception of the teaching of STEM subjects. Indeed, as a result of this increased awareness, there has been a noticeable change in the education system, as is evident by programs implemented by the Division of Science and Technology in the Ministry of Education.

Dr. Ofer Rimon, Head of the Division of Science and Technology, explains (Katz 2011):

> In the T&B ('Technician & Bagrut [matriculation])' program, students study until the end of the twelfth grade and earn both Bagrut (matriculation) and Technician certificates. They study subjects that are relevant to the economy in which there is a shortage of technicians and practical engineers (electronics, mechanical engineering, electricity and computers).
>
> The program Integrating Students in Industry is designed for students, that concerns are expressed with respect to their chances to obtain a matriculation certificate upon completing their studies. In this program, students work in workshops and factories once or twice a week where, in a real technological environment, they learn the secrets of technology. The program ensures their employment horizon on the one hand, and on the other hand, opens possibilities for their post-high school studies (beyond Technician and Practical Engineer).

4.2.4 Risk Category: Study Sequences—School, Higher Education, Military, Labor Market

This risk category represents the point of view of the other stakeholders, from the IDF, the industry and the academia. The risk factors identified in this category relate to the importance of continuity and connectivity between school education and the higher education system, the army and the labor market. This category also emphasizes the importance that these stakeholders attribute to STEM education, since the shortages of skilled human resources harm the organizations they serve.

The risk factors grouped in the category (Table 4.6) reflect the procedural barrier in the education system.

Table 4.6 Study sequences—the procedural barrier and risk factors

Barrier	Risk factors
Procedural barrier	21. Long training is needed to prepare high school graduates for technological jobs in the military service
	22. Shortage of engineers in the industry*
	23. Shortage of practical engineers and technicians in the industry*
	24. Shortage of skilled low-tech professionals in the industry
	25. Lack of career plan programs for high school students
	26. Universities are required to offer preparatory courses for high school graduates before accepting them to undergraduate science and engineering studies to close gaps in the STEM subjects

*The reviewed risk factors are starred

Risk factors 22 and 23: Shortage of engineers, practical engineers, and technicians in the industry

A National Economic Council report (Levin 2012) indicates a low supply of skilled human resources, which is not sufficient for the needs of the industry. The shortage hits the industry and Israel economic growth in general, and the growth of the high-tech sector in particular. The report informed about 6195 vacancies of scientist and engineers in the fields of high technology (system analysis, computer science, electrical and electronic engineering, computer engineering, engineer and electrician, electronics, machinery) and practical computer technicians and programmers. At that time, high-tech professions accounted for about 41% of all vacancies academic occupation in Israel. In addition, the report emphasizes that the business sector facing shortages of skilled human resources at a high level mainly in the areas of computing: computer science, computer engineering, and electronics, with a special focus on R&D positions.

The stakeholders described the procedural barrier as a lack of coordination between the education system and the labor market in relation to the demand of graduates in the STEM subjects.

L., representative of the high-tech industry, ties between the industry's shortage of engineers and the reduction of the percentages of high school graduates in STEM studies over the last decade. She also emphasizes the need for the graduates of universities in the fields of engineering and their importance for the high-tech companies due to their high research capabilities:

> We know that every year 4500 students graduate in the engineering field in all the Israeli universities and colleges in Israel … the increment in the number of students enrolled to colleges is 10% per year and in universities—only by 1% per year, if at all. For us, this causes a critical problem since students who are universities graduates do research… The high-tech industry needs about 7000 employees per year and the increment in demand is about 6% every year, so if you calculate, you see that the gap is growing.

4.2.5 Risk Category: Management of STEM Education

This category describes the following two perceptions:

- The STEM teachers' perspective: Their attitudes relate to weaknesses and threats which result from the bureaucratic-professional conflict, which was demonstrated in two conflicts: The academic freedom conflict and the profession perception conflict.
- The other STEM stakeholders' perspective: Their attitudes describe the economic barrier (the limited budget appointed to technology education in Israel) and the procedural barrier (the involvement of military and industrial entities in the processes of teaching in high school).

These conflicts and barriers are expressed by the risk factors listed in Table 4.7.

Risk factors 27 and 31: Tight supervision over teachers and principals and Parents' involvement in schools

The more a system is rigid, the more rules it dictates and the less academic freedom it provides to the professionals. Hall (1968) points out that a major component of professionalism is the demand for autonomy and for professional commitment. In particular, two conflicts are expressed in relation to the risk factors mentioned above: the academic freedom conflict and the profession perception conflict.

T., a Math teacher, expresses the STEM teachers' aspirations for academic freedom mainly by reducing the pedagogical supervision of the organization:

> More freedom should be given. I think it's very depressing that you're told exactly what to do every day. Even on the level of which exercise to do in class and which to do at home… It really doesn't let you develop any creativity… first of all, give the teacher more freedom in structuring his [or her] own teaching and professionalism.

Table 4.7 Management of STEM education—conflicts, barriers, and risk factors

Conflicts	Barriers	Risk factors
Academic freedom conflict Profession perception conflict	Procedural barrier Economic barrier	27. Tight supervision over teachers and principals*
		28. Bureaucratic work is required from principals and teachers
		29. School success is measured by the eligibility of a matriculation certificate and not by the subjects included in the certificate
		30. Lax discipline in schools
		31. Parents' involvement in schools*
		32. Involvement of military and industry in STEM education in the high school*
		33. Limited budget to open technology classes

*The reviewed risk factors are starred

The profession perception conflict is illustrated very well by the involvement of the principal (and parents) in the STEM teachers' work. Clearly, the principal is the ultimate authority at the school and is, naturally, subject to external influences (organizational policies, parental pressure, etc.). However, the principal authority may clash sometimes with the professional position of the STEM teachers. Such principal–teacher conflicts ignore the teachers' need for professional autonomy, professional devotion, and faith in self-supervision.

Oplatka (2007) describes the conflict as follows: "According to the traditional hierarchical structure, the principal is the final arbiter; however, he is not an expert in every subject taught in the school. Although the principal bears responsibility for pedagogical-didactic matters as well, he must cooperate with the teachers, who are perceived as professionals and as authorities in the pedagogical decision-making process at school. An administrative approach that emphasizes the principal's authority as derived from his position in the hierarchy, may encounter opposition within the school."

M., a Math subject coordinator in a high school, describes this clash as follows:

> The headmaster is a very nice person, to the extent of saying 'yes' after others have already said 'no'. At the end of the day, this is insulting. As the Math coordinator, I informed my decision to assign a student to the 3-unit level [a low level of studying Mathematics], whereas the parents wanted the student to be in four [unit of studying Mathematics, where 5 units is the advanced level]; or, he may be in the four-unit level and the parents want him to be in five… The pressure is then ratcheted up, and eventually reaches the principal, and he says 'yes'.

Risk factor 32: Involvement of military and industry in STEM education in the high school

Global trends in recent decades, resulting from the spread of neoliberal perceptions in the economy of Western countries, point at the reducing role of governments in providing public services and the privatization of services previously granted by the state. In education, these trends led to increased involvement of external agents (Schiffer et al. 2010), mainly with respect to issues related to social gaps and equal opportunities and mobility (Ben-Ami 2008). However, the participation of such agents in educational processes could jeopardize the identity, core values, and objectives of the education system due to their loyalty to goals that serve the organizations they represent (Brinkerhoff 2002).

A., a representative of philanthropic organization, which promotes STEM education in Israel, explains form the nonprofits NGOs' perspective, the challenge her organization faces when it is involved in the implementation of programs in the education system:

> We have to say the word 'interests' when it comes to philanthropy, there are interests. Now I have a donor who wants to promote national identity … or one who wants to work only with female students [on promoting STEM studies]. … The tension between the interests, opportunities and risks is very big … It is a challenge, but when there is a national goal, you strengthen it.

The STEM stakeholders involved in promoting STEM education in the education system pointed at the suspicious and tense relationships with the education sector and at the bureaucracy involved in the process of implementing new programs. Such relationships raise the discussion about how to promote and manage multi-sectoral partnership in STEM education. The common perception is that the education system should be public and responsible for the educational agenda. The study participants, however, claim that a policy of *institutional partnership* with second and third sectors should be promoted (Schiffer et al. 2010). This policy preserves the role of the public sector, in our case, the education system, as the body in charge of public education in the country. However, at the same time, it provides some degree of controlled decentralization that enables other sectors to participate in the educational activities in line with the goals of the education system (see Sects. 6.3.4 and 6.4).

4.2.6 Risk Category: Social Perceptions

This risk category represents the perspective of executives from the education system and of stakeholders from the industry and military sectors. The risk factors in this category relate to the social perception of science studies and to the diminished image of technology education. Consequently, executives from the education system express the threat with respect to the opening of technology education tracks in the schools, while the stakeholders from the industry and the military refer to the impact of these social perceptions on the shortage of STEM graduates needed for the organizations they represent. Table 4.8 presents the risk factors in this category.

Table 4.8 Social perceptions—barriers and risk factors

Barriers	Risk factors
Psychological-personal barrier Sociocultural barrier	34. Negative labeling of vocational education*
	35. Vocational jobs are not valued*
	36. The perception "I am not qualified for studying science subjects" is common among students*
	37. The perception "It is better to study easier subjects" is common among students*
	38. The perception "Vocational education is associated with social gaps in the Israeli society" is common in the public*

*The reviewed risk factors are starred

Risk factors 34, 35, and 38: Negative labeling of vocational education; vocational jobs are not valued; and the common perception that vocational education is associated with social gaps in the Israeli society

The percentage of high school students who currently study in the technology education tracks in Israel is lower than it was in the past. In 2012, about 40% of all high school students participated in these tracks, in contrast to the end of the 70s, when 52% of high school students in Israel learned in the technology education (when it was called vocational education). This percentage includes the three tracks: engineering, technology, and occupational (see the Terminology chapter). Specifically, while the Israel's traditional industries face shortage of graduates of the technology and occupational tracks, the high-tech industries need graduates of the engineering track. Testimonies of these shortages are heard occasionally by representatives of the second sector.

Dr. Tal Lotan, representative of the Manufacturers Association of Israel (MAI),[9] addressed these shortages in a discussion about STEM education in Israel, that took place at the Committee of Science and Technology of the Knesset (the Israel representative house), on July 15, 2015:

> From 2010, we examine the needs of the industry: 80% of the employers claim they have difficulty recruiting skilled workers over the years in the whole spectrum. The industry's need for manpower is unreasonable: We're talking about engineers in the field of machinery, electrical and electronic; we are talking about engineers, electricians, we're talking about mechanics, locksmiths. … That is, where ever we touch, we meet the shortage of manpower and this shortage becomes critic over the years. It is not only the budget cut in the technology education; it is also as a result of a low status.

Risk factors 36 and 37: Students' common perceptions: "I am not qualified for studying science subjects" and "It is better to study easier subjects"

The psychological-personal barrier in this context expresses students' (and their parents') perceptions about the study of the science subjects. School principals explained that students perceive the science studies as "very difficult" and avoid choosing them since they perceive themselves as not capable enough for these studies.

G. is the director of the high school supervision division of a local authority, who is also a physic teacher. He expresses the psychological-personal brier and highlights the influence of parents and society in this context:

> Often students give up because they do not want to work hard. The parents do not want to be the authority and do not direct the kids… they give up… in a high socio-economic communities parents join the reluctance of the child, [in order] not to confront with [the kid]. Parents say: "Leave the kid now, he will learn after the military service… It is important for me that he will gain positive experiences… he is a social activist, a scout coach, I want him to perceive himself positively". In fact, the friends are those who eventually direct the student to study science at the advanced level.

---

[9]The MAI website is http://www.industry.org.il/Eng/.

4.2.7 *Risk Category: National Programs in STEM Education*

This risk category expresses the point of view of the stakeholders of STEM education, who refer to the threats of the frequent changes in national programs due to government turnover, which affect also the other sectors in Israel. The risk factors in this category reflect the political barrier (due to the frequent government turnover) and the procedural barrier expressed in difficulties in the implementation of reforms (Havelock and Huberman 1977).

Table 4.9 presents the risk factors in this category.

Risk factors 40, 41, and 43: Lack of teacher training process prior the implementation of a new national program; Lack of persistence in the implementation of long-term national programs; and Implementation of national programs without appropriate infrastructure

The political barrier is expressed in the lack of future long-term planning, together with the failure to establish a measurement and control system which fit such plans. In fact, the frequent changes of government and, consequently, the political need for immediate output, usually lead to a situation in which long-term planning is suppressed. A., a regional supervisor of a school network, describes:

> This change in policy is very fast, also in the policy of the Ministers of Education. Frequent changes do not allow learning from mistakes or from successes and future planning is also missing… For example, the excellence programs [for scientific and technological studies] was an important element of the system and now it suddenly stopped. Will it continue or not? Who knows?… It started three years ago. How could it be stuck? What they have already achieved?

In the same spirit, educational researchers, who analyze success of educational reforms, also refer to the same weakness. Slavin's (in Cuban 1990) explains this phenomenon by the fact that policy makers do not conduct research and sincere evaluations about the effectiveness of their plans before they are implemented.

Table 4.9 National programs—barriers and risk factors

Barriers	Risk factors
Procedural barrier Political barrier	39. The introduction of new national programs reduces the importance attributed to previous national programs
	40. Lack of teacher training process prior the implementation of a new national program*
	41. Lack of persistence in the implementation of long-term national programs*
	42. Budgets for infrastructure, teaching and training hours are increased especially when a crisis is identified
	43. Implementation of national programs without appropriate infrastructure*

*The reviewed risk factors are starred

This finding was found also in another research conducted recently in Israel about research-practice partnerships in STEM education in Israel (Hazzan et al. 2016).

4.3 Summary

In this chapter, we review seven risk categories of STEM education in Israel:

- Sectors in STEM education
- Teachers—opportunities, training, and social status
- Curriculum of STEM subjects
- Study sequences—school, higher education, military, labor market
- Management of STEM education
- Social perceptions
- National programs in STEM education.

These categories represent 43 risk factors identified in Phase A of our study.

As can be seen, a risk management process in general, and the risk identification phase presented in this chapter in particular, can be nicely applied also for the field of STEM education. Indeed, these 43 risk factors could have been identified without a risk identification process (and in that case would have been probably called "problems" or "challenges" rather than risk factors). However, the wider context of risk management, in which our work has been conducted, not only provided the education system many points of reference to learn from, it also fostered the education system to take a proactive approach, as is illustrated in the next chapters.

References

Argyris, C. & Schön, D. (1978) *Organizational learning: A theory of action perspective,* Reading, Mass: Addison Wesley.

Barak, M. (2011). Improvement of teacher quality by organizational-oriented policy, the whole (school) is bigger than the sum of its parts (teachers). *Hed Hachinuch 86*(1), 29–30 (Hebrew). http://portal.macam.ac.il/ArticlePage.aspx?id=4471

Ben-Ami, G. (2008). Parent's selection of education and the theme of equal opportunities, *E-mago – Culture and Contents Magazine* (Hebrew). http://www.e-mago.co.il/Editor/edu-2517.htm

Brinkerhoff, J. M. (2002). Government-nonprofit partnership: A defining framework. *Public administration and development, 22*(1), 19–30.

Chen, D. (2005). School as a "learning organization". The Ministry of Education website (Hebrew). http://cms.education.gov.il/EducationCMS/Units/Nisuyim/Meyda/

Cuban, L. (1990). Reforming again, again and again. *Educational Researcher, 19*(1), 3–13.

Dovrat, S. (2005). *The National Task Force for the Promotion of Education in Israel.* The Ministry of Education, Israel. (Hebrew)

Hall, R. H. (1967). Some organizational considerations in the professional-organizational relationship. *Administrative Science Quarterly, 12*(3), 461–478.

Hall, R. H. (1968). Professionalization and Bureaucratization. *American Sociological Review, 33* (1), 92–104.

Hativa, N. (December 2008). Is teaching a profession?, *Hed Hachinuch* (Hebrew). http://www.itu.org.il/?CategoryID=1476&ArticleID=12506&Page=1

Havelock, R.G. & Huberman, A. M. (1977). *Solving Educational problems – The Theory and Reality of Innovation in Developing Countries.* IBE Studies and Surveys in Comparative Education, Paris: UNESCO.

Hazzan, O., Heyd-Metzuyanim, E. & Dori, Y. J. (unpublished report, 2016). Research-Practice Partnerships in STEM education: An organizational perspective.

Katz, S. (April, 2011). The Importance of technology education in Israel has recognized: Interview with Dr. Ofer Rimon - Head of the Division of Science & Technology at the Ministry of Education, *Kesher Ayin* (*Eye Contact*) *Monthly Magazine* (Hebrew). http://cms.education.gov.il/EducationCMS/Units/MadaTech/HinucMadaTech/MeidaPirsumim/tikshoret/Matkshoret.htm

Levin, H. (2012). *The Shortage in Skilled Human Resources in the High-Tech Industry*, The National Economic Council, The Ministry of Prime Minister. http://www.pmo.gov.il/Lists/FAQkalkala/Attachments/21/tech.pdf

Oplatka, Y. (2007). The Foundations of Education Administration: Leadership and Management in the Educational Organization, Pardes Publications (Hebrew).

Schiffer, V., Berkovitz, Y., Bar-Yehuda, S., & Almog-Bareket, G. (2010). *The Involvement of Third Sector Organizations in the Education system – White Paper*, Van-Leer Institute, Jerusalem (Hebrew). http://www.vanleer.org.il/sites/files/product-pdf/73-sFileRedir.pdf

Chapter 5
Phase B: Risk Rating

Abstract This chapter describes the rating of the risk factors of STEM education in Israel. Data were collected by a Delphi survey in which 186 practitioners, from the five stakeholder groups from all sectors of the Israeli society, participated. The 43 risk factors identified in Phase A (Chap. 4) were ranked by three levels of severity (high, medium, and low) (Mikes and Kaplan 2014). This phase emphasizes *strategic risks* which endanger the objectives of the organization in general and in our case—the objectives of STEM education in Israel.

Keywords Risk management · STEM education · Risk rating · Levels of severity · Strategic risks

5.1 The "Risk Management—Risk Rating" Questionnaire

Risk management theory attributes importance to the process of risk assessment, that is, risk evaluation and ranking (IRM 2002). This process in a business enterprise is conducted by examining the likelihood and impact of the identified risks (see Sect. 2.4).

In our study, which examined the perceptions of STEM teachers and stakeholders with respect to risk management of STEM education in Israel, a risk rating process was conducted by using a Delphi survey (see Sect. 2.3 and Research process—Sect. 3.2.4). In this phase, the Risk management—Risk rating questionnaire was designed, data was collected and analyzed, and 15 significant risk factors were elicited. This questionnaire enabled to identify *strategic risks* that reflect *social perceptions* in the Israeli society. This process is described in what follows.

A. Even Zahav and O. Hazzan, *Risk Management of Education Systems*,
SpringerBriefs in Education, DOI 10.1007/978-3-319-51984-5_5

5.1.1 The "Risk Management—Risk Rating" Questionnaire Formulation

The URL of the questionnaire is https://docs.google.com/forms/d/e/1FAIpQLSdlkdw3Smkoc2_FggUCAWzPY4U_fnlX8L0PAJB5clG_7qrGmA/viewform.

In what follows, we present its main characteristics.

- The same question was asked with respect to each of the 43 risk factors. The question was: "For each characteristic, please rank (on a 1–4 scale) your estimation with respect to the severity of its implications on STEM education in the broadest sense." The term "broadest sense" was added since some of the risk factors may have direct implications for other sectors, beyond STEM education (e.g., risk factor 22-shortage of engineers in the industry).
- A Likert Scale of 1–4 was used (1—No severity, 4—High severity) since (a) it is simple to choose from a small number of severity levels; (b) the even number of severity levels requires to take a position, either below or above a neutral assessment (since a neutral option is not provided).
- Space for open-ended responses was given to allow the participants to share explanations, reasoning, and thoughts. This data was analyzed qualitatively and enabled to understand the choice of the severity level.
- In addition to the above Likert Scale, two additional options were given:
  - "Advantage": In case a participant does not consider a factor as a risk, but rather as an advantage of STEM education in Israel;
  - "Unfamiliar": In case a stakeholder is not familiar with the risk factor. This option was relevant since the participants belonged to different sectors. For example, participants from the education system are more familiar with risk factors related to the curricula, while participants from the other stakeholder groups may not be familiar with them.
- A brief explanation about the questionnaire was presented at the top of the questionnaire and concepts that required clarification were explained.
- The questionnaire was not divided into sections and all the 43 risk factors were visible simultaneously. This presentation allows rolling the questionnaire back and forth.
- The participants were asked to fill in several personal details; nevertheless, it was not mandatory to fill them in. The only required question in this section was "To what sector of STEM education does you current organization belong? This question is required for our data analysis." This question was mandatory since it enabled us to analyze the data according to the five groups of stakeholders (Fig. 5.1).
- Following a thorough validation process (by ten research participants from five stakeholders groups, three researchers in STEM education, and two statistician), 18 risk factors which received a low score were eliminated from the questionnaire and several formulations of risk factors were improved. At the end of the

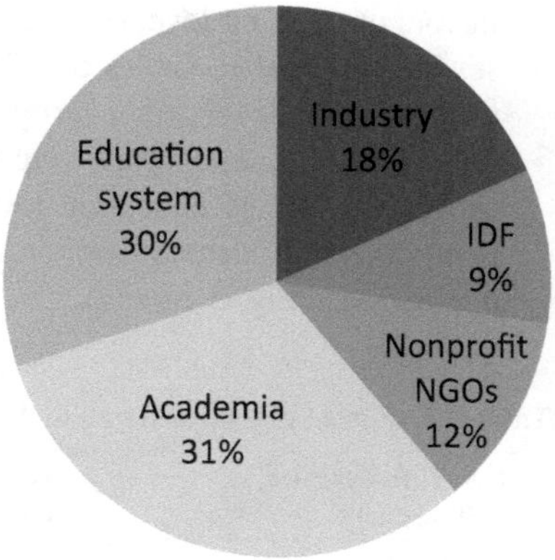

Fig. 5.1 Distribution of the respondents by sector

process, the questionnaire included 43 risk factors grouped in seven risk categories (Sect. 4.2).

In addition, the participants were asked to rate the seven risk categories according to the severity of their implications on STEM education (Sect. 5.2.3).

5.1.2 The "Risk Management—Risk Rating" Questionnaire Distribution

The questionnaire was distributed during three months on electronic media to 400 representatives from five stakeholder groups. Response was received from 186 representatives. Figure 5.1 shows the distribution of the respondents by sector.

5.1.3 The "Risk Management—Risk Rating" Questionnaire Analysis

Data were analyzed in several steps:

- For each risk factor, the following measures were calculated: average score, standard deviation, median, mode, and the number of times the risk factor was specified as "Unfamiliar" or "Advantage."
- Table 5.4 presents the criteria for determining the level of severity for each risk factor. According to these criteria, the 43 risk factors were sorted into three levels of severity: 15 risk factors[1] of high level of severity—Level 3, 18 risk

[1]We highlight at this point that most of the 15 risk factors that were highly rated relate to what we shall call later *strategic risks*.

factors of medium level of severity—Level 2, and 10 risk factors of low level of severity—Level 1. Tables 5.1, 5.2, and 5.3 present the 43 risk factors according to these three levels of severity of their implication.

- The seven risk categories were rating according to the severity of their implications on STEM education (Sect. 5.2.3). Two categories were ranked higher than others: Teachers—opportunities, training, and social status and Social perceptions (Fig. 5.3).

Table 5.1 Fifteen risk factors with high severity level

Category: risk factors (# in Table 4.1)	Average score	SD	Median	Mode	Advantage	Unfamiliar
1. Teachers[a]: the teaching profession is not appreciated by the public (8)	3.74	0.6	4	4	0	2
2. Teachers: many teachers who teach science in elementary school lack education in the field (12)	3.7	0.58	4	4	2	11
3. Teachers: STEM teachers' salary is low relative to alternatives jobs in the industry (9)	3.63	0.65	4	4	1	7
4. Teachers: the working conditions of STEM teachers are not attractive (10)	3.59	0.64	4	4	1	14
5. National programs: lack of persistence in the implementation of long-term national programs (41)	3.67	0.56	4	4	0	19
6. National programs: implementation of national programs without appropriate infrastructure (43)	3.61	0.62	4	4	1	10
7. National programs: budgets for infrastructure, teaching, and training hours are increased especially when a crisis is identified (42)	3.53	0.63	4	4	4	15
8. National programs: lack of teacher training process prior the implementation of a new national program (40)	3.5	0.72	4	4	1	33
9. Sectors: male students in ultraorthodox schools do not study STEM subjects at all (2)	3.54	0.74	4	4	0	18
10. Management[b]: limited budget to open technology classes (33)	3.54	0.7	4	4	1	16
11. Social perceptions: vocational jobs are not valued (35)	3.53	0.71	4	4	0	2

(continued)

Table 5.1 (continued)

Category: risk factors (# in Table 4.1)	Average score	SD	Median	Mode	Advantage	Unfamiliar
12. Social perceptions: negative labeling of vocational education (34)	3.52	0.71	4	4	1	7
13. Social perceptions: the perception "It is better to study easier subjects" is common among students (37)	3.5	0.66	4	4	0	10
14. Social perceptions: the perception "I am not qualified for studying science subjects" is common among students (36)	3.48[c]	0.66	4	4	1	10
15. Study sequences[d]: shortage of practical engineers and technicians in the industry (23)	3.48[e]	0.68	4	4	5	13

[a]The risk category "Teachers—opportunities, training and social status" appears in this chapter in short as "Teachers" in Tables, Figures and additional explanations
[b]The risk category "Management of STEM education" appears in this chapter in short as "Management" in Tables, Figures and additional explanations
[c]The score 3.48 was round up to 3.5
[d]The risk category: "Study sequences—school, higher education, military, labor market" appears in this chapter in short as "Study sequences" in Tables, Figures, and additional explanations
[e]The score 3.48 was round up to 3.5

Table 5.2 Eighteen risk factors with medium severity level

Category: risk factors (# in Table 4.1)	Average score	SD	Median	Mode	Advantage	Unfamiliar
1. Teachers: placement and guidance of novice STEM teachers is not provided (11)	3.38	0.78	4	4	2	29
2. Lack of promotion tracks for STEM teachers (7)	3.36	0.75	4	4	1	19
3. Teachers: only small number of junior high school teachers who teach "Science and Technology" are Physics or Chemistry teachers (13)	3.28	0.78	3	4	4	15
4. Teachers: number of students who study STEM education in universities is low (14)	3.24	0.82	3	4	1	11
5. Teachers: lack of a collaborative professional	3.14	0.81	3	3	0	28

(continued)

Table 5.2 (continued)

Category: risk factors (# in Table 4.1)	Average score	SD	Median	Mode	Advantage	Unfamiliar
community for STEM teachers (15)						
6. Study sequences: shortage of engineers in the industry (22)	3.44	0.73	4	4	7	11
7. Study sequences: shortage of skilled low-tech professionals in the industry (24)	3.38	0.78	4	4	2	13
8. Study sequences: lack of career plan programs for high school students (25)	3.2	0.9	4	4	3	12
9. Management: lax discipline in schools (30)	3.39	0.8	4	4	0	4
10. Management: school success is measured by the eligibility of a matriculation certificate and not by the subjects included in the certificate (29)	3.16	0.87	3	4	4	8
11. Management: bureaucratic work is required from principals and teachers (28)	3.1	0.85	3	4	1	1
12. Management: parents' involvement in schools (31)	3.1	0.87	3	4	9	8
13. Sectors: most of the ultraorthodox female students do not study science subjects on the advanced level in high school (1)	3.34	0.77	3	4	0	20
14. Sectors: if a female student faces difficulty in learning advanced science subject, there is a tendency to suggest her to study the subject on a lower level (6)	3.2	0.94	3	4	0	10
15. Social perceptions: the perception "Vocational education is associated with social gaps in the Israeli society" is common in the public (38)	3.26	0.88	3	4	3	22

(continued)

Table 5.2 (continued)

Category: risk factors (# in Table 4.1)	Average score	SD	Median	Mode	Advantage	Unfamiliar
16. Curriculum: the curriculum of the vocational education subjects does not match the needs of the labor market (19)	3.04	0.9	3	3	6	15
17. Curriculum: the teaching of STEM subjects focuses mainly on the preparation toward the matriculation exams (20)	3.02	0.94	3	4	18	12
18. Curriculum: technological aspects are not sufficiently integrated in science studied in the elementary school (16)	2.96	0.88	3	3	1	17

Table 5.3 Ten risk factors with low severity level

Category: risk factors (# in Table 4.1)	Average score	SD	Median	Mode	Advantage	Unfamiliar
1. Sectors: many students attending vocational education are associated with social-economic periphery (4)	2.93	0.89	3	3	13	15
2. Sectors: percentage of students studying advanced level science subjects among male students is higher than among female students (5)	2.88	0.91	3	3	4	4
3. Sectors: many students attending military classes are associated with social-economic periphery (3)	2.38	0.94	2	2	28	32
4. National programs: the introduction of new national programs reduces the importance attributed to previous national programs (39)	2.68	0.95	3	3	5	70
5. Curriculum: structure and content of STEM education in junior high schools: the	2.9	0.94	3	3	23	17

(continued)

Table 5.3 (continued)

Category: risk factors (# in Table 4.1)	Average score	SD	Median	Mode	Advantage	Unfamiliar
subject "Science and Technology" is taught as one block of four disciplines (Biology, Chemistry, Physics, and Technology) (17)						
6. Curriculum: frequent changes in the curricula of STEM subjects (18)	2.82	0.98	3	3	14	20
7. Study sequences: universities are required to offer preparatory courses for high school graduates before accepting them to undergraduate science and engineering studies to close gaps in the STEM subjects (26)	2.6	0.97	3	3	31	6
8. Study sequences: long training is needed to prepare high school graduates for technological jobs in the military service (21)	2.4	0.99	3	3	28	46
9. Management: tight supervision over teachers and principals (27)	2.48	0.94	2	2	46	44
10. Management: involvement of military and industry in STEM education in the high school (32)	2.8	0.98	3	3	69	15

Findings of this phase were consistent with the data analysis conducted in Phase C—Risk Response Phase, in which the "Risk management—re-rating and response" questionnaire was distributed.

5.2 Finding: Risks Rating—Identification of Significant Risks for STEM Education in Israel

The findings of the Rating Phase (Phase B) will be presented as follows:

(a) The score analysis of the 43 risk factors (Sect. 5.2.1);
(b) Grouping the risk factors by three levels of severity: High, medium, and low (Sect. 5.2.2);
(c) Rating of the risk categories (Sect. 5.2.3).

5.2.1 The Scores of the 43 Risk Factors

This section presents a quantitative analysis of the "Risk management—Risk rating" questionnaire,[2] which was completed by 186 research participants. One of the measures indicated for each risk factor is the average scores on a scale of 1–4 (1—No severity, 4—High severity). As can be seen in Fig. 5.2, the average score of 15 risk factors is equal or greater than 3.5. Figure 5.2 also indicates for each risk factor the standard deviation of its ratings.

Furthermore, Fig. 5.2 indicates three risk categories that their risk factors rated relatively high: Category 2—Teachers; Category 6—Social perceptions; and Category 7—National programs. In addition, the averages values of the risk factors in these categories reflect uniformity (that is, the differences in the average scores of the risk factors in these categories are similar). This observation was further supported by the next step of the data analysis in which the risk factors were categorized into three levels of severity: High, medium, and low, by additional measures (Sect. 5.2.2).

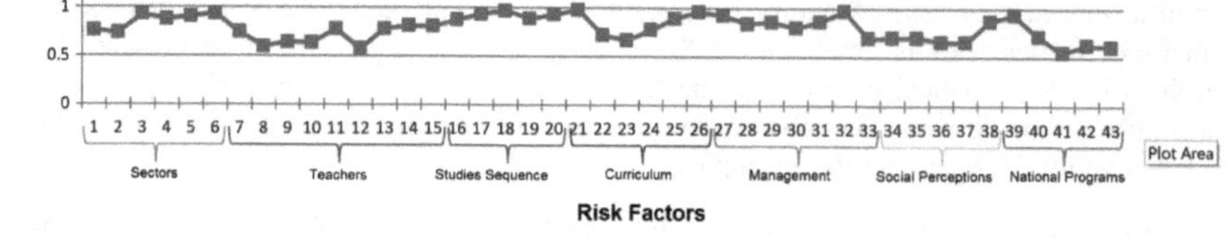

Fig. 5.2 Averages and standard deviations of risks factors

[2]See https://docs.google.com/forms/d/e/1FAIpQLSdlkdw3Smkoc2_FggUCAWzPY4U_fnlX8L0PAJB5clG_7qrGmA/viewform.

5.2.2 Grouping the Risk Factors by Three Levels of Severity: High, Medium, and Low

Based on the consideration of additional statistical measures, the 43 risk factors were grouped into three levels of severity:

(a) 15 risk factors with high severity levels (Table 5.1)
(b) 18 risk factors with medium severity level (Table 5.2)
(c) 10 risk factors with low severity level (Table 5.3).

In more details, the grouping of the 43 risk factors into three levels of severity was based on the consideration of several indicators of descriptive statistics: Average, standard deviation, median, and mode. Also, for each risk factor, it was checked if the number of respondents who chose one of the two options: "Advantage" or "Unfamiliar" was small relative to the said risk's average score.[3] Tables 5.1, 5.2, and 5.3 shows these indicators for each risk factor.

Table 5.4 indicates how the severity level is determined according to these indicators. These criteria are listed below:

Table 5.4 Criteria for selecting risk severity levels

Criteria severity level	Average	Standard deviation	Median	Mode	# of risk factors
High	3.5–4	0–0.6	4	4	15
Medium	2.95–3.5	0.6–0.8	3 or 4	3 or 4	18
Low	2–2.95	More than 0.8	1, 2 or 3	1, 2 or 3	10

[3]As it turns out, in most cases, the number of participants who marked these options for a specific risk factor correlated with its severity level. Specifically, for risk factors, whose severity level was determined by the statistical indicators to be "high," these two options where chosen by a very small number of participant. This observation was found to be applicable also for the other two levels of severity. Here are several examples:

- For risk factor 8, which was ranked on a High severity level, "Advantage" was not selected at all, and "Unfamiliar" was selected by two participants (Table 5.1).
- For risk factor 20, which was ranked on a Medium severity level, "Advantage" was selected by 18 participants and "Unfamiliar"—by 12 participants (see Table 5.2).
- For risk factors, 21, 27, 39, whose severity level was determined to be low, these options were selected as follows: "Advantage"—28, 46 and 5 and "Unfamiliar"—26, 44 and 70, respectively, (Table 5.3).

This fact further validated the assigned severity level of a given risk by the statistical indicators.

1. An average score bigger than 3.5 on the ranting scale of 1–4 was determined high;
2. A small standard deviation indicates uniformity of the rating values. Therefore, a standard deviation smaller than 0.6 indicated an agreement among participants;
3. The median and the mode also indicate the score uniformly. For example, mode 4 indicates that the majority of respondents selected 4 for the severity of the risk factor. Therefore, the value 4 was chosen for the median and for the mode as an indicator for a high level of severity of a risk factor.

If a risk factor meets at least three of the four criteria of a severity level as is indicated in Table 5.4, it was classified to the said severity level.

In what follows, we explain the rationale for the high severity rating of the 15 risk factors presented in Table 5.1. We explain the risk factors according to the number of risk factors per category.

- The risk factors in the "*teachers*" category—# 1, 3, and 4 in Table 5.1 or # 8, 9, and 10 in Table 4.1—describe characteristics associated with choosing the teaching profession: External benefits, such as wage and working conditions, alongside with social benefits, such as the society's recognition of the teacher's professional status. Indeed, social benefits are known as a major factor that plays a role in choosing the teaching profession (Oplatka 2007). Thus, the perception in the Israeli society of the teacher's status is considered a risk that offends STEM educational goals—the necessity to increase the number of qualified applicants who turn to teach STEM subjects (Sects. 2.4 and 3.1, Period D—the 2000s). The additional risk factor belonging to the Teachers category is "Many teachers who teach science in elementary school lack education in the field" (# 2 in Table 5.1 or # 12 in Table 4.1). It reflects the importance attributed by the research participants to adequate teachers' training and STEM knowledge.
- The risk factors in the "*National programs*" category—# 5, 6, 7, and 8 in Table 5.1 or # 41, 43, 42, and 40 in Table 4.1—describe the implications of the frequent changes that take place in national STEM education programs. New programs immediately effect the education system, since the implementation of a new national program requires teacher training and sometimes also pedagogical and operational infrastructure. These risk factors may harm the success of the implementation of the said programs and are considered as risk factors associated with political barriers (Havelock and Huberman 1977) in general and with high and frequent turnover of Ministries of Education in Israel in the last decade in particular (Sect. 4.1.2).
- Risk factors in the "*Social perceptions*" category—# 11, 12, 13, and 14 in Table 5.1 or # 35, 34, 37, and 36 in Table 4.1—reflect perceptions in the Israeli society related to the public image of vocational education (# 11 and 12 in

Table 5.1) and students' self-perception related to science subjects. Students' perceptions about their capability and ability (# 13 and 14 in Table 5.1) reflect their perception whether they will effectively cope with problems, work in an unfamiliar environments and attain achievements (Deci and Ryan 2008). This low self-esteem regarding success in science subjects prevents students from choosing studying science subject in the high school (Hannover and Kessels 2004). In turn, this social perceptions harm the achieving of the goals of STEM education, among them, increase in the number of students who choose STEM subjects by attracting students from underrepresented sectors in Israel in the science subjects.

- The risk factor in the "*Sectors*" category—# 9 in Table 5.1 or # 2 in Table 4.1—addresses one such underrepresented group in STEM studies in Israel. Specifically, it addresses the importance attributed to the participation of the ultraorthodox sector in the job market in general and in professions which require STEM studies in particular.
- The risk factor which appears in the "*Management*" category—# 10 in Table 5.1 or # 33 in Table 4.1—deals with the limited budget allocated for technology classes and reflects an economic barrier (Sect. 4.1.2).
- The risk factor in the "*Study sequences*" category—# 15 in Table 5.1 or # 23 in Table 4.1—explains the participant's concern related to choosing the scientific professions (# 13 and 14 in Table 5.1). The lack of choosing science subjects in the high school has direct implication on the number of students who choose studying science and engineering disciplines in higher education and the profession of practical engineers and technicians, both are in high demand in the Israeli high-tech industry.

Table 5.5 presents the number of risk factors by their categories and severity levels.

Table 5.5 Number of risk factors by their categories and severity levels

Risk category	High	Medium	Low	Total
Teachers	4	5		9
Social perceptions	4	1		5
National programs	4		1	5
Curriculum		3	2	5
Management	1	4	2	7
Sectors	1	2	3	6
Study sequences	1	3	2	6
Total	15	18	10	43

5.2.3 *Risk Categories Rating by Their Severity Impact on STEM Education in Israel*

The study participants were also asked to choose the risk categories whose severity impact is the highest[4]. More than one category could be chosen. The rating of the risk categories according to these responses is presented in Fig. 5.3.

As can be seen from Fig. 5.3, the Teachers category, to which the highest number of risk factors belong (Table 5.5), was ranked significantly higher relative to the other categories: 50% of the respondents indicated it as one of the most severe category. Also, the "Social perceptions" category was indicated as one of the most severe category by 35% of respondents. The other categories were selected as most sever categories as follows: 26% selected the "National programs" category, 25%—the "Curriculum" category, 24%—the "Management" category, 19%—the "Sectors" category, and finally, 12% of the respondents indicated the "Study sequences" as one of the most severe category.

The ranking of the risk categories according to the severity of their implications on STEM education in Israel highlights the two relatively highly ranked categories: "Teachers—opportunities, training, and social status" and "Social perceptions." The ranking of these categories as severe risk categories indicates the importance the research participants attribute to STEM teachers—whose professional opportunities, training, and professional status, and to risks associated with social perceptions regarding STEM education. The implications of these categories are indeed crucial for the achievement of the goals of STEM education in Israel:

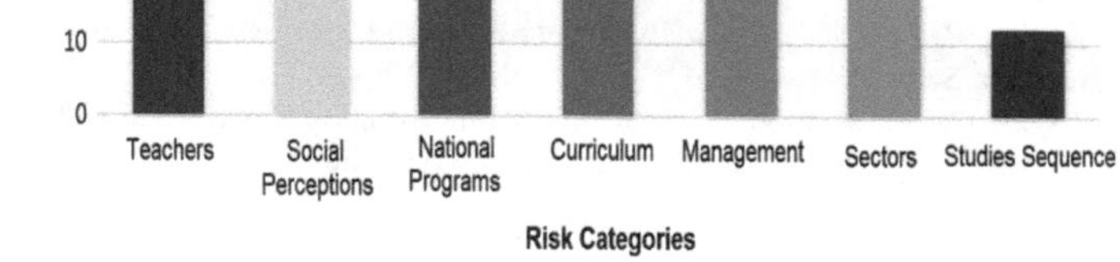

Fig. 5.3 Risk categories ranking

[4]The question was formulated as follows: "In your opinion, what are the categories whose severity level is the highest? At least one category should be chosen.*" That is, the participants could choose the number of categories they consider as categories severity level is the highest. Also, this question was mandatory.

See https://docs.google.com/forms/d/e/1FAIpQLSdlkdw3Smkoc2_FggUCAWzPY4U_fnlX8L0PAJB5clG_7qrGmA/viewform.

Increasing the number of graduates in the STEM subjects and, in accordance, increasing the number of quality STEM teachers (see Sects. 2.4 and 3.1, Period D—the 2000s).

5.3 Summary

This chapter presented the risk rating of the risks of STEM education in Israel, as conceived by the research participants. Many of the risks, whose severity level was rated high, belong to the Teachers and Social perceptions categories. Specifically, these risk factors reflect perceptions in the Israeli society regarding the status of the teaching profession and regarding STEM education. Since they threaten STEM education in Israel from achieving its goals, they are considered as *strategic risks* (Mikes and Kaplan 2014). This analysis indicates the centrality of strategic risks. Accordingly, the response plan (Phase C—Chap. 6) presents courses of action for coping with these *strategic risks*, while dealing with additional risks.

References

Deci, E. L. & Ryan, R. M. (2008). Hedonia, eudaimonia, and well-being: An introduction. *Journal of Happiness Studies* **9**(1), 1–11.

Hannover, B. & Kessels, U. (2004). Self-to-prototype matching as a strategy for making academic choices. Why high school students do not like math and science. *Learning and instruction* **14** (1), 51–67.

Havelock, R.G. & Huberman, A. M. (1977). *Solving Educational problems – The Theory and Reality of Innovation in Developing Countries.* IBE Studies and Surveys in Comparative Education, Paris: UNESCO.

IRM (2002). *Risk Management Standard.* The Institute of Risk Management (IRM), The Association of Insurance and Risk Managers (AIRMIC) and the National Forum for Risk Management in the Public Sector (ALARM). https://www.theirm.org/media/886059/ARMS_2002_IRM.pdf.

Mikes, A. & Kaplan, R. S. (2014). *Towards a contingency theory of enterprise risk management.* Harvard Business School.

Oplatka, Y. (2007). The Foundations of Education Administration: Leadership and Management in the Educational Organization, Pardes Publications (Hebrew).

Chapter 6
Phase C: Risk Response

Abstract In this chapter, we propose a response plan mainly for the *strategic* risks, while addressing also the *operational* and *external* risks. Thirteen courses of action are proposed: Five courses of actions are internal to the education system; eight courses of actions involve cooperation with stakeholders from other sectors in Israel. Data was gathered in focus groups in which stakeholders of STEM education participated. The discussion on the focus groups concentrated on how to reduce the impact of the strategic risks. Among them, a cross-sectoral cooperation has been largely suggested, discussed, and analyzed. Accordingly, we present frameworks related to forms of cross-sectoral collaboration in general and in STEM education in particular.

Keywords Risk management · STEM education · Response plan · Strategic risks · Courses of action · Focus groups · Cross-sectoral cooperation

6.1 Introduction to the Response Phase: Operational Risks, Strategic Risks, and External Risks

In a business organization, this phase concludes the risk management process. In this phase, a response plan is presented, and a risk mitigation plan is being applied for the risks identified and rated in the previous phases (IRM 2002). In addition, at this phase, strategies for exploiting opportunities, identified at the first phase of the risk management process—the identification phase—are considered. These strategies are implemented together with the risk mitigation strategies (Hillson 2001; Ben Israel and Kuns 2013).

As stated, the study presented in this Brief implemented a risk management process for STEM education in Israel that resembles the process as it is carried out in business organizations. At the identification and rating phases, risk factors that reflect *perceptions of the Israeli society* were identified and highlighted, respectively. Specifically: (a) the public recognition of teachers in Israel and (b) the attitude toward STEM education in Israel. The ranking phase elicited the risk factors that were rated "high" with respect to the severity of their implication on the goals set by the system of STEM education.

A. Even Zahav and O. Hazzan, *Risk Management of Education Systems*, SpringerBriefs in Education, DOI 10.1007/978-3-319-51984-5_6

It is important to note that *in the context of business organizations, social perceptions are not defined* usually *as risks. In our context, that is, STEM education, their identification as risk factor on high severity level reflect the significance of the society in risk management processes of education systems*. Accordingly, the response phase presented in this chapter offers how to mitigate them both by internal courses of action of the education system and by collaboration with stakeholders of STEM education from other sectors.

In this study, we chose the categorization framework suggested by Mikes and Kaplan (2014), which offers a framework for business organizations for managing their risks. This risk categorization framework sorts risks into three levels according to the difficulties involved in their elimination: from the easy level (1) to the difficult level (3).

Level 1: These are *operational risks* related to internal issues and processes of the organization and are often made by mistakes or accidentally. These risks are preventable, and therefore, are perceived as easy to deal with.

Level 2: These are *strategic risks* that may jeopardize the achievement of the organization's goals, but, at the same time, their mere existence may produce profit for the organization. These risks are associated with the organization's type of operation. For example, companies operating in hazardous industries, such as mines, oil and gas, or other companies, such as high-tech companies, pharmaceutical industries, medical equipment, and aerospace industry, should be involved in high-risk projects for their actual product development. Therefore, the way these risks are managed may effect their likelihood and impact, but a remnant of these risks will always exist. Therefore, they are considered as risks on a medium level.

Level 3: These are *external risks*, which are caused by unpredictable events, on which the organization does not have any control, and therefore, has to accept their existence. Some of these risks exist as a result of the organization's strategic objectives and its activities, and therefore are related to strategic risks (e.g., mergers and acquisitions, expansion of target markets, and geographical expansion). Consequently, they can be only partly controlled and are effected by a high uncertain and uncontrollable dimension. This category also includes political changes, regulation, and competitive environments. In this case, though these risks are excluded from the immediate control of the organization, the organization should be ready for their appearance. In general, these risks are treated as risks that it is difficult to eliminate.

In contrast to a business organization, the education system is a nonprofit public organization. Therefore, this categorization framework was adopted in our study to the case of STEM education as follows.

Level 1—Operational risks: Similar to Mikes and Kaplan's (2014) definition, operational risks are internal to the organization and, in our case represent administrative and operational weaknesses of STEM education in Israel. At this level, most of the risk factors belong to the following risk categories: Teachers[1]; Management of STEM education; Curriculum; and Study sequences. These risks

[1]Risk factors from the teachers category were classified into two types of risks:

have been identified as a consequence of the *bureaucratic-professional conflict* that STEM teachers face and of *procedural barriers* of STEM education expressed in change management processes in STEM education (see Chap. 4). Accordingly, as a response to these operational risks, the stakeholders suggested a common strategy, that is, *Avoid*[2]—remove them completely.

Level 2—Strategic risks: Similarly to Mikes and Kaplan's (2014) definition, these risks threaten the achievement of the goals of STEM education in Israel, including: increasing the number of students who learn STEM subjects, increasing the number of teachers respectively, and improving the teaching quality. In our study, strategic risks reflect perceptions in the Israeli society regarding science subjects and vocational education, the status of the teaching profession, and sectors in the Israeli society. As strategic risks, the organization must deal with them proactively in order to mitigate them. According to the stakeholders' perceptions, the proposed response strategy for these risks is *Mitigate*, that is, act to reduce the chance of their likelihood and their impact, in order to minimize the damage to the objectives of STEM education in Israel.

Level 3—External risks: Similarly to Mikes and Kaplan's (2014) definition, these risks were identified as risks related to the external environment of the education system that the organization cannot treat them and should accept them. The risk factors identified as external risks for STEM education are *economic and political barriers* related to the implementation of national programs in STEM education and the budget allocated for STEM education. The education system should develop resilience and define a policy in case these risk factors will actualize. In other words, means of dealing with these risks should be sought, but the response strategy for coping with them is *Accept*.

Based on this framework, the risk factors identified in Phase A were recategorized according to a common theme and type of risk: operational, strategic, or external. The new gathering yielded 10 main *Risks* (to distinguish from Risk Factors) for STEM education in Israel, as described below.

- **3 Operational risks**:
  - Teachers: Promotion and training
  - Intra-organization management and control
  - Study sequences and connectivity to the job market.
- **4 Strategic risks**:
  - Negative perceptions regarding science subjects

(Footnote 1 continued)

- Risk factors which describe operational weaknesses, such as, teachers training and professional promotion, were classified as operational risks;
- risk factors, which describe the perception of the teaching profession status, were classified as strategic risks.

[2]See Sect. 2.4 the risk response strategies.

- Public image of technology education
- The social status of the teaching profession in the Israeli society
- Sectoral gaps.

- **3 External risks**:
  - Teachers' salary
  - Technology education budget
  - Implementation of national programs in STEM education.

Table 6.1 presents the 10 risks and the 43 risk factors (presented in Phase A, Chapter 4, Table 4.1) associated with each risk.[3] Table 6.1 presents also the following data:

a. The severity level of each risk factor (1—low, 2—medium, 3—high), as ranked in Phase B—Risk Rating (see Tables 5.1, 5.2, 5.3, and 5.4);
b. Risk severity for each of the 10 risks, which is the average of the rating of the risk factors associated with the risk;
c. Weight of the risk type—operational, strategic, and external—which is the sum of the severity scores of the risks associated with the risk type.

The next section presents the response plan by treating the 10 risks of STEM education according to the three types of risks: operational, strategical, and external.

6.2 Response Plan

In most cases, the strategic risks enjoy top priority since they directly effect the achievement of the organization's goals. Similarly, in our case, the focus of the proposed response plan is the strategic risks, due to their high ranking by the research participants vis-à-vis the severity of their impact on the goals of STEM education (see Table 6.1).

The response plan for risk management of STEM education also addresses the operational and the external risks. Specifically, since interrelationships exist between risks, that is, dealing with one risk effects other risks, the response plan proposes to *mitigate* the strategic risks by *avoiding* operational risks and *accepting* external ones. In addition, the response plan implements the *exploit* strategy for opportunities (see Sect. 2.4), by suggesting to collaborate with stakeholders while

[3]In the recategorization process conducted in Phase C, the risk factors were disconnected from the risk categories identified at Phase A. For example, Category 2 "Teachers - opportunities, training and social status," identified in Phase A, composes of both external risks and strategic risks. Thus, Risk factor 9: "STEM teachers' salary is low relative to alternatives jobs in the industry," is associated in the recategorization to the external risk "Teachers' salary", and Risk factor 8: "The teaching profession is not appreciated by the public," is associated in the recategorization to the external risk "Public image of technology education."

Table 6.1 Ten risks of STEM education in Israel

Risk type	The risk	Risk factors (RF) and their ranking by level[a]
Operational Risks Weight 5.36 (Sum of the scores of the 3 operational risks: 2.2 + 1.66 + 1.5 = 5.36)	Teachers: Promotion and training Risk severity: 2.2	1. Lack of promotion tracks for STEM teachers (RF 7) (2) 2. Placement and guidance of novice STEM teachers is not provided (RF 11) (2) 3. Many teachers who teach science in elementary school lack education in the field (RF 12) (3) 4. Only small number of junior high school teachers who teach "Science and Technology" are Physics or Chemistry teachers (RF 13) (2) 5. Lack of a collaborative professional community for STEM teachers (RF 15) (2)
	Intra-organization management and control Risk severity: 1.66	6. Tight supervision over teachers and principals (RF 27) (1) 7. Bureaucratic work is required from principals and teachers (RF 28) (2) 8. School success is measured by the eligibility of a matriculation certificate and not by the subjects included in the certificate (RF 29) (2) 9. Lax discipline in schools (RF 30) (2) 10. Parents' involvement in schools (RF 31) (2) 11. Involvement of military and industry in STEM education in the high school (RF 32) (1)
	Study sequences and connectivity to the job market Risk severity: 1.5	12. Technological aspects are not sufficiently integrated in science studied in the elementary school (RF 16) (2) 13. The structure and content of STEM education in junior high schools: The subject "Science and Technology" is taught as one block of four disciplines (Biology, Chemistry, Physics and technology) (RF 17) (1) 14. Frequent changes in the curricula of STEM subjects (RF 18) (1)

(continued)

Table 6.1 (continued)

Risk type	The risk	Risk factors (RF) and their ranking by level[a]
		15. The curriculum of the vocational education subjects does not match the needs of the labor market (RF 19) (2) 16. The teaching of STEM subjects focuses mainly on the preparation toward the matriculation exams (RF 20) (2) 17. Long training is needed to prepare high school graduates for technological jobs in the military service (RF 21) (1) 18. Lack of career plan programs for high school students (RF 25) (2) 19. Universities are required to offer preparatory courses for high school graduates before accepting them to undergraduate science and engineering studies to close gaps in the STEM subjects (RF 26) (1)
Strategic Risks Weight: 9.42 (Sum of the scores of the 4 strategic risks: 2.66 + 2.6 + 2.5 + 1.66 = 9.42)	Negative perceptions regarding science subjects Risk severity: 2.66	20. The perception "I am not qualified for studying science subjects" is common among students (RF 36) (3) 21. The perception "It is better to study easier subjects" is common among students (RF 37) (3) 22. Shortage of engineers in the industry (RF 22) (2)
	Public image of technology education Risk severity: 2.6	23. Negative labeling of vocational education (RF 34) (3) 24. Vocational jobs are not valued (RF 35) (3) 25. The perception "Vocational education is associated with social gaps in the Israeli society" is common in the public (RF 38) (2) 26. Shortage of practical engineers and technicians in the industry (RF 23) (3) 27. Shortage of skilled low-tech professionals in the industry (RF 24) (2)

(continued)

Table 6.1 (continued)

Risk type	The risk	Risk factors (RF) and their ranking by level[a]
	The social status of the teaching profession in the Israeli society Risk severity: 2.5	28. The teaching profession is not appreciated by the public (RF 8) (3) 29. Number of students who study STEM education in universities is low (RF 14) (2)
	Sectoral gaps Risk severity: 1.66	30. Most of the ultraorthodox female students do not study science subjects on the advanced level in high school (RF 1) (2) 31. Male students in ultraorthodox schools do not study STEM subjects at all (RF 2) (3) 32. Many students attending military classes are associated with social-economic periphery (RF 3) (1) 33. Many students attending vocational education are associated with social-economic periphery (RF 4) (1) 34. Percentage of students studying advanced level science subjects among male students is higher than among female students (RF 5) (1) 35. If a female student faces difficulty in learning advanced science subject, there is a tendency to suggest her to study the subject on a lower level (RF 6) (2)
External Risks Weight: 8.6 (Sum of the scores of the 3 external risks: 3 + 3 + 2.6 = 8.6)	Teachers' salary Risk severity: 3	36. STEM teachers' salary is low relative to alternatives jobs in the industry (RF 9) (3) 37. The working conditions of STEM teachers are not attractive (RF 10) (3)
	Technology education budget Risk severity: 3	38. Limited budget to open technology classes (RF 33) (3)
	Implementation of national programs in STEM education Risk severity: 2.6	39. The introduction of new national programs reduces the importance attributed to previous national programs (RF 39) (1) 40. Lack of teacher training process prior the implementation of a new national program (RF 40) (3)

(continued)

Table 6.1 (continued)

Risk type	The risk	Risk factors (RF) and their ranking by level[a]
		41. Lack of persistence in the implementation of long-term national programs (RF 41) (3) 42. Budgets for infrastructure, teaching and training hours are increased especially when a crisis is identified (RF 42) (3) 43. Implementation of national programs without appropriate infrastructure (RF 43) (3)

[a]Alongside each risk factor, two parentheses appear
– its original number (as given in Phase A, Table 4.1, where RF means risk factor)
– its severity ranking (as determined according to Table 5.4; presented also in Tables 5.1, 5.2 and 5.3)

treating the risks. This opportunity is derived from the social recognition of the importance of STEM education for Israel society and economy.

Figure 6.1 describes schematically the response plan.

- The different colors indicate the three types of risks: green—operational, yellow—strategical, red—external.
- The rectangle size represents the different weights of the risk types (Table 6.1). As can be seen, indeed, the weight of the strategic risks is the biggest among the three types of risks.
- The three risk types are presented on two axes: the X axis represents the difficulty level of dealing with the risk (1—low, 2—medium, 3—high—see the beginning of this section); the Y axis represents the risk severity.[4] As can be seen, the severity of the external risks is the highest among the three types of risks.

Furthermore, Fig. 6.1 shows that

- The courses of action suggested by the participants to "*Avoid operational* risks" and "*Accept external* risks" foster, in turn, the implementation of the *Mitigation* strategies for the *strategic* risks.

[4]The severity of the operational, strategic, and external risks (as types of risks) was calculated by converting their weights (Table 6.1) to a 1–3 scale. For example, the weight of the strategic risks was converted from 4 to 12 range (4—if all risks were rated 1; 12—if all risks rated 3) to 1–3 range: (9.42/12) × 3 = 2.35. Similarly, the severity of the external and operational risks was converted from 3–9 range to 1–3 values range to (8.6/9) × 3 = 2.87 and (5.36/9) × 3 = 1.78, respectively.

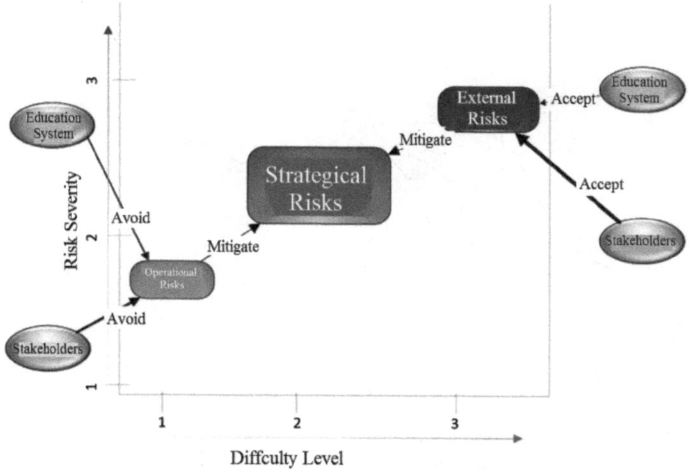

Fig. 6.1 Response plan for risk management of STEM education in Israel

- Both the "*Avoid* operational risks" and the "*Accept* External risks" strategies are treated in two ways: internally by the education system and externally, through its collaboration with stakeholders of STEM education in other sectors.
- In both cases, more courses of action are based on collaborations with stakeholders of STEM education, than on actions promoted by the education system itself.[5] The courses of action are presented in the Sect. 6.3.

Figure 6.2 zooms in Fig. 6.1, presenting the 10 risks of STEM education (Table 6.1). Similarly to Fig. 6.1, the severity levels and difficulty levels of dealing with them are presented on two axes (1—low, 2—medium, 3—high).[6] The arrows represent 13 courses of action suggested by the stakeholders to mitigate the strategic risks to which the arrow points, by either avoiding the operational risks or accepting the external risks. The number on the arrow represents the number of the course of action as it appears in Table 6.2. The number on the arrow represents the number of the course of action as it appears in Table 6.2. Figure 6.2 clearly shows the connections of the four strategic risks to the other risks and thus, highlights their centrality.

Figure 6.2 and Table 6.2 presents 13 courses of action to *mitigate* the following four strategic risks: The social status of the teaching profession in the Israeli society; Public image of technology education; Negative perceptions regarding

[5]The thicker an arrow is, the bigger the number of courses of action suggested to deal with the risk the arrow points to is.

[6]The severity is expressed both by the height on the severity axis and the rhombus size. We decided to reflect the severity level of a risk in two ways in order also to visualize the comparative relations between the 10 risks.

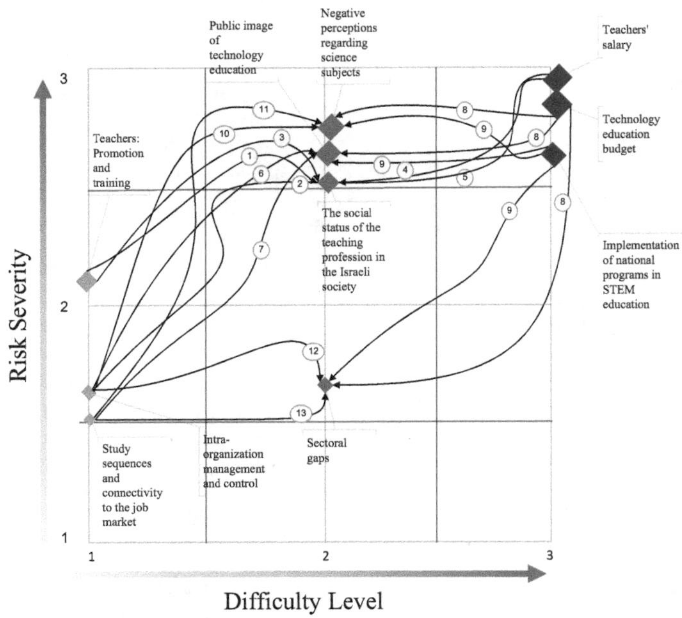

Fig. 6.2 Mapping of STEM education risks in Israel

science subjects; Sectoral gaps. The *mitigation* of these risks is suggested either in two approaches: "*Avoid* operational risks" or "*Accept* external risks."

In addition:

- The courses of action for dealing with the strategic risks suggest exploiting the opportunity of collaboration with stakeholders of STEM education from other sectors in Israel.
- The number of the suggested courses of action for dealing with risks based on a collaboration with stakeholders of STEM education in Israel is higher than the number of suggested courses of action suggested for dealing with risks only by the education system (8 vs. 5 respectively).
- Several courses of action mitigate more than one strategic risk.
- For each course of action, we also specify the operational or external risks that it either avoids or accepts, respectively (see Table 6.2, in parentheses).

6.3 Four Strategic Risks and 13 Courses of Action

The response plan suggests 13 courses of action. Five courses of action are suggested to be carried out by the education system and eight courses of action are suggested to be carried out by collaborations with stakeholders of STEM education in Israel (see Table 6.2 and Fig. 6.3).

Table 6.2 Courses of action for mitigating the strategic risks

Strategic Risks	*Avoid* operational risks		*Accept* external risks		Total[b]
Carried out by	the education system	cooperation with stakeholders	the education system	cooperation with stakeholders	
The social status of the teaching profession in the Israeli society	1. Teacher training, career development, and guidance (Operational risk: Teachers: Promotion and training) 2. Autonomy, trust, and supervision discharge (Operational risks: Intra-organization management and control)	3. STEM teachers' mobility (Operational risk: Teachers: Promotion and training)	4. Salary equalization between novice and senior teachers (External risk: Teachers' salary)	5. Integrated earning (External risk: Teachers' salary)	5
Public image of technology education	6. Clear messages concerning the importance of technology education (Operational risk: Intra-organization management and control)	7. Appealing learning material and career advising (Operational risk: Study sequences and connectivity to the job market)		8. Increasing budget with the assistance of for-profit and nonprofit organizations[c] (External risk: Technology education budget) 9. Establishment of a national council for STEM education (External risk: Implementation of national programs in STEM education)	4
Negative perceptions regarding science subjects	10. Nurturing the ability and capability among male and female students (Operational risk: Intra-organization management and control)	11. Exposing students to high-tech representatives and organizations (Operational risk: Study sequences and connectivity to the labor market)		Courses of action 8 and 9: Suggested regarding the risk "Public image of technology education" education	4

(continued)

Table 6.2 (continued)

Strategic Risks	*Avoid* operational risks		*Accept* external risks		Total[b]
Carried out by	the education system	cooperation with stakeholders	the education system	cooperation with stakeholders	
Sectoral gaps		12. Established cooperation with for-profit and nonprofit organizations (Operational risk: Intra-organization management and control) 13. Inclusion of sectors which are partly represented in STEM education (Operational risk: Study sequences and connectivity to the labor market)		Courses of action 8 and 9: Suggested regarding the risk "Public image of technology education" education	4
Total courses of action: —8 based on a collaboration with stakeholders —5 to be carried out by the education system	4	5	1	3	

[a]The courses of action are numbered
[b]The sum of this column is bigger than 13 since several courses of action are applied for more than one strategy
[c]Courses of action 8 and 9 can mitigate also the strategic risks "Negative perceptions regarding science subject" and "Sectoral gaps"

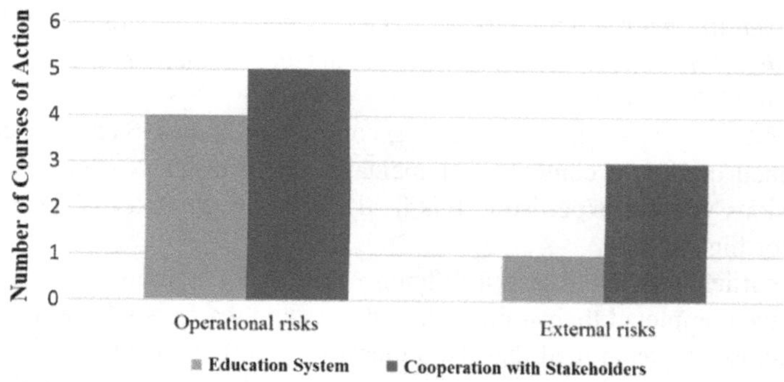

Fig. 6.3 Dealing with risks of STEM education in Israel—Education system and cooperation with stakeholders

In the next sections, the 13 courses of action are described according to the four strategic risks[7]:

- Strategic risk 1: The social status of the teaching profession in the Israeli society—Courses of action 1–5
- Strategic risk 2: Public image of technology education—Courses of action 6–9
- Strategic risk 3: Negative perceptions regarding science subjects—Courses of action 10–11
- Strategic risk 4: Sectoral gaps—Courses of action 12–13.

6.3.1 Strategic Risk 1: The Social Status of the Teaching Profession in Israel

Five courses of action are suggested (Courses of action 1–5) for coping with this risk.

Course of action 1: Teacher training, career development, and guidance
Study participants pointed out a clear association between the social status of the teaching profession and the need to improve teachers' training and advancement. Three themes brought up in this context.

[7]The response plan for the strategic risk "The social status of the teaching profession in the Israeli society" is presented first, though its severity is lower than the severity of Strategic risks 2 and 3, since it was largely addressed by the research participants, and accordingly, the highest suggestions for coping with it were proposed by the research participants. The ways of dealing with the strategic risk "Public image of technology education" are presented before the ways which deal with the strategic risk "Negative perceptions regarding science subjects" because the number of risk factors associated with risk factor 2 is higher than the number of risk factors associated with risk factor 3 (5 and 3 respectively).

a. *Increment in the requirements for STEM teachers training, specifically for professional training of elementary school science teachers and STEM teachers in junior high schools.*
The need for enforcement the training component among STEM teachers was mentioned mainly in context of elementary school teachers who teach science professions without expertise in this field and in the context of STEM teachers in junior high school.
Study participants noted also a difference in teacher training between teachers who have completed their training in colleges and teachers who were trained in universities. It was argued that the admission conditions for teacher colleges in Israel are low, which may harm the professional skills of the graduates and accordingly the status of the teacher profession.
The participants argued that an increase in the level of admissions, not only will contribute to the quality of teaching, but will also improve teachers' status both among students and among their parents. They based their proposal based on the experienced gained in other countries, such as Singapore and Finland.
In Finland, the consideration of teacher status as a risk that may actualize one day was taken into account at the beginning of the 70s. As a response, the admission requirements to the teaching profession were raised and teacher training was reshaped, turning into a research-oriented study program. Eventually, the risk has been removed. Sahlberg (2011) describes the current situation in Finland as follows:

> Teacher training in Finland is also recognized because of its systematic and research-based structure. All graduating teachers, by the nature of their degree, have completed research-based masters' theses accompanied by rigorous academic requirements of theory, methodology and critical reflection equal to any other field of study in Finnish universities at that level. (p. 94).

b. *Professional development options for post-elementary teachers.*
The need to provide teachers options for professional development in the teaching career is supported by the theory of personal well-being at work, which attributes importance to the fulfillment of the individual's aspirations in the organization (Deci and Ryan 2008). In the context of STEM teachers, our study identified their desire for advancement in the *professional* aspect of their teaching career, rather than in the administrative/managerial aspect (as is possible by dual ladder promotion processes). L., a Chemistry teacher describes her personal ambitions for professional advancement:

> To do something beyond teaching… do things that promote… if I could, I would have done more things that effect… trying to do something that will bring additional solutions on the national level but also to improve teaching methods and ways of thinking that are important to me… to go out to colleges, become a head of a department, these options are very interesting.

c. *Implementation of mentoring programs for teachers in their first teaching years in order to cope with the high rate of teacher drop out.*

In order to reduce teacher drop out in the first years of teaching, it was suggested to provide pedagogical support and guidance system for new teachers who join the education system.

Recently, efforts are being made in Israel to include a guidance program for new teachers as part of the teacher training programs. In the 2015–2016 academic year, a national program, called "Academia-Class" was launched. In this program, prospective teachers in their third year of study, join an experienced teacher in the school for 12–16 weekly hours, serve as additional classroom teacher, and work side by side with a the mentor teacher. The program is based on an Irish program and is one of the recommendations of the EU for improving quality of teachers and their training (European commission 2013).

In conclusion, according to the research participants, teachers' status maybe improved by raising the requirements of STEM teachers training program, opening professional development options for post-elementary STEM teachers, and guiding new teachers in the first years of teaching.

Course of action 2: Autonomy, trust, and supervision discharge

Providing academic freedom and autonomy to teachers, while decreasing the supervision of their work, may increase teachers' trust and public recognition both by the education system and by the society in Israel.

S., a principal of a post-elementary school, describes her expectation for trust which will be reflected in reduced level of supervision when new programs are implemented:

> There are too many supervisors and implementers of different programs… Say what your expectations are and leave us. If we need, we will ask for help… believe in us. Help a school that does not meet the requirements, that doesn't have what you consider as essential.

Indeed, studies identified that social rewards, such as the society's recognition of the professional status of teachers, and granting autonomy related to their professional freedom, are top priority motives for choosing the teaching profession (Oplatka 2007).

Course of action 3: STEM teachers' mobility

This course of action describes STEM teachers' mobility between sectors—education and industry. It fosters the idea that the STEM teachers are capable to integrate work both in the education system and in the industry.

In recent years, the education system employs STEM teachers with previous professional background as scientists and engineers in the high-tech industry. This process may improve the status of the teaching profession, since these teachers have high-quality professional knowledge as well as a variety of professional—management and research—skills.

Teachers of STEM subjects who integrate work in the industry with work in the education system expressed their satisfaction form the combination of the two worlds. H., a part-time high school teacher of space sciences, describes this experience:

I combine challenging work [at the high-tech] together with a job that grants me personal satisfaction.

This course of action can be implemented based on collaborative relationships of the education system with industrial organizations. On the one hand, willingness and flexibility is required from the education system to enable such a structure of the teaching position. On the other hand, the industry may encourage its employees to study for a teaching certificate in one of the STEM subjects and contribute in a part-time position to STEM education in Israel.

Course of action 4: Salary equalization between novice and senior teachers
Data about teachers' salaries in Israel indicate that teachers' salaries have been increased in the last decade. The increase of teachers' salaries, began with the implementation of the reforms "Ofek Hadash" (New Horizon) and "Oz Latmura" (Power to the Change), which changed the structure of the teaching position in order to increase the quality of teaching. However, the salary increase was expressed mainly for senior teachers, whose salaries today are higher by about 30% than the average salaries in the labor market and are almost equal to the salary level of other university graduates (OECD 2015).

However, the salaries gap between senior (ages 55–64) and novice (ages 25–34) teachers is higher: A senior teacher earns 2.1 times more than a novice teacher. Furthermore, when salaries of Israeli teachers are compared with the salaries of their peers at the OECD countries, big gaps are identified. The average salary of teachers in the OECD countries is 1.7 times higher than the average salary of high school teachers in Israel. For example, consider two teachers with a similar level of education and 15 years of teaching experience: the teacher from Finland earns 1.8 times more than the Israeli teacher, the teacher from the USA earn 2.3 times more, and the teacher from Luxembourg—4.3 times (OECD 2015).

Teachers' salaries constitute a threat of STEM education since it effects the future work of STEM teachers in the education system and the recruitment of new teachers. This threat was raised by STEM teachers at the risk identification phase and its severity was ranked high, along with the conditions of teachers' employment. Nevertheless, this risk can neither be avoided nor removed, since it depends on salary balances determined for government employees in Israel as a whole.

The study participants suggested different ways to mitigate the risk of teachers' salary. For example, for teachers with previous experience in the industry, it was suggested to approve their seniority level based on their experience in the industry. Indeed, these teachers, who join the education system after years of industry experience, bring with them technical and management skills gained in their professional career. Their added value to the education system is high and may improve the status of the teaching profession in Israel in general and the quality of STEM teaching in particular.

Based on this recognition, the Ministry of Education established a process that fosters the approval of previous professional experience of STEM teachers who had worked in the industry as scientists and engineers before they switched to education.

Course of action 5: Integrated earning
This course of action is closely related to courses of action # 3 and 4. This course of action proposes to improve teachers' income by part-time employment in the industry. This action may also encourage qualified and experienced scientist and engineers, who work in the industry and wish to be involved in the education system, to join the education system, since it allows them to keep higher earnings and at the same time to fulfill their desire for teaching.

6.3.2 Strategic Risk 2: Public Image of Technology Education

Four courses of action are suggested (Courses of action 6–9) for coping with this risk.

Course of action 6: Clear messages concerning the importance of technology education
The findings of the identification phase indicated the absence of clear messages regarding the importance of STEM education in general and the technology education tracks in particular, either by interior school officials or by the education system as a whole. For example, the education system measures high school success according to the percentage of students who complete the high school studying with a matriculation diploma and not by the diploma content; as a result, school principals do not encourage excellence in STEM subjects. Clear messages related to the importance of STEM subjects, delivered by the organization's management may encourage students to choose STEM courses in general and technology courses in particular.

This is how Y., a mechanical engineering teacher, describes the vague messages delivered by his school management with respect to the engineering tracks:

> It is simple lack of attention from the principals… inappropriate attention to the subjects of the engineering profession, maybe some attention is given to Electronics, but nothing to my field of Mechanical Engineering … I have a theory that I couldn't prove by research, but it is different when the school management doesn't have background in technological discipline… In our school the background of the entire management is history, Bible [and] literature disciplines.

The conjecture presented by Y. about principals' background and the attention they give to STEM education in the schools, has been investigated in the first stages of our study by a questionnaire that was distributed to the schools whose teachers participated in the study. Interestingly, out of 10 school principals, only two principals had academic background in STEM professions (Mechanical Engineering and Biology). This hypothesis has to be validated with a larger sample in order to deepen our understanding about how the professional background of the principals is expressed in the attention they give and the importance they attribute to the STEM subjects in their school.

Course of action 7: Appealing learning material and career advising
This action suggests to teach in the high school study programs which follow the pace of technological progress, present employment opportunities, and demonstrate the practice of their studies and their relevance to current developments in the industry.

This idea was emphasized in a focus group in which stakeholders from for-profit and nonprofit organizations, including STEM teachers, participated. These representatives suggested to adopt the strategy *Exploit* for opportunities, in our case, exploit the recognition of the industry in Israel with respect to the importance of STEM education, and establish cross-sector cooperative initiatives. Several ways were offered for the promotion of such cooperative initiatives:

a. Build attractive study programs: The study participants noted that it is not sufficient to market the technology courses by lectures and advanced laboratories in schools. Rather, students and parents should gain some hands-on experience that shows the change that occurred in vocational education when it was transformed to technology education.
b. Create a career advisement programs: Such a program should help students choose the direction of their future employment based on the understanding of the future labor market in general and what professions are relevant for the future in particular. The education system in Finland creates such a curricula in line with expected predications related to the labor market in Finland in 2025 that helps students in choosing future career direction (Hanhijoki et al. 2012). In addition, career consultation program has been introduced at the junior high school level.

Course of action 8: Increasing budget with the assistance of for-profit and nonprofit organizations
Budget increase will enable to open upgraded technology labs and classrooms that allows hands-on learning experience. These labs may attract students to join the technology education tracks in the school: engineering, technology, and occupational tracks (see the Terminology section at the beginning of the Brief). This course of action suggests to partner for this purpose with both for-profit and non-profit NGOs.

Course of action 9: Establishment of a national council for STEM education
The education system in Israel is tightly effected by the political system. Replacement of Ministries of Education after the elections often leads to the establishment of new national programs by the new Minister of Education.

This course of action suggested to deal with the frequent changes of national programs by the establishment of a National Council for Education in general and for STEM education in particular. The idea is based on the National Education Act (1953), which regulates the education system. According to this National Education

Act, an education committee should be established with at least 15 members, appointed for a period of four years by the Minister of Education and approved by the government. According to this 60-years-old law, members of the Committee include representatives from the field of education, the Ministry of Education, higher education institutions, and teacher organizations. Based on this regulation, an attempt was made to establish this education council in the tenure of the last three Israeli governments (Weissblei 2013). However, the process has not been completed.

The study participants conceive STEM education as a national infrastructure and economic engine for the state of Israel and highlight the importance of such body that will define policy and long-term strategy for the education system.

This line of thinking is reflected in the following quote of Haim Rousso, a member of the National Council for Research and Development Committee. Mr. Rousso presented his perspective in 2015, in a meeting of the Knesset Committee of Science and Technology which discussed STEM education in Israel.

> The problem is that our system is not stable. Education system is a system with long time constants, nothing is happening in two years, this is about the average tenure of a minister. That's how we roll from one idea to the next idea, one time steering the wheel to the right, sometimes steering the wheel to the left and nothing happens. I think that till we introduce stability into this system we will just continue talking… We probably won't succeed affecting the length of ministers' service, it's probably not under our control, but I do think we can apply existing models in the education system. … We need to establish a [national council], I mean at least for technology education… especially for the technology education system which is much more dynamic, because of the frequent changes, it must have a Council.

6.3.3 Strategic Risk 3: Negative Perceptions Regarding Science Subjects

Two courses of action are suggested (Courses of action 10 and 11) for coping with this risk.

Course of action 10: Nurturing the ability and capability among male and female students

As mentioned earlier, the science subjects—the advanced level of Mathematics, Physics, Chemistry, Computer Science and Biology—are convinced by students as more difficult than other subjects, and therefore, students tend not to choose them as their elective in the high school. Specifically, the study identified perceptions related to the high difficulty level students ascribe to the science subjects, such as: "I'm not qualified to study science" and "it is better to study easier subjects." Participants noted the development of negative perceptions in relation to the science subject from an early age (elementary school and junior high school) and associated this phenomenon with the teaching quality at these levels due to lack of teacher knowledge in the science subjects.

M., Director of the municipal project demands from the subject coordinators to "fight" for every student:

> Children give up, parents give up, I [the teacher] discourage them because it depends on my message delivered to them: Why do you need to learn at the 5 units [advanced] level? You can always complete it. [With] such messages you [the teacher] can convince the pupil to move [to low-level study]. … my tendency is to work less hard. Why should I work hard? Everyone are happy: the teacher is pleased because he works less hard, he has excellent students who get high scores, his work is "evident", the student is satisfied, parents are satisfied that the child is happy and relaxed and doesn't need private lessons, the principal is pleased that he has quiet in the school and he can show excellence [high percentages of students with a matriculation diploma]. So if everyone is happy, and if it is so good, then what's wrong? … My role now … I'm trying to take care of this phenomenon and I demand from the subject matter coordinators to make an effort… to foster the ability of each student.

Course of action 11: Exposing students to high-tech representatives and organizations

The importance of exposing students to new fields in the industry in Israel, as an incentive for students to choose in technology education tracks (specifically the engineering track), was expressed by the study participants. Among other things, activities that combine visits in high-tech industries in Israel, meetings with scientists in their workplace, and science museums tours, were mentioned.

Study participants noted that though these activities exist today, in most cases, they are local initiatives promoted by teachers and principals and are funded by the local authority or by the parents. It was proposed to integrate these frameworks as part of the studies of the STEM subjects, so that it will be directed by the education system.

Cooperation with the business sector is also important and may contribute to the attractiveness of the science subjects and students' selection of these subjects as interesting fields of occupation in the future. Specifically, recognizing the importance of increasing the number of graduates in the STEM subjects alongside organizations' demand for CSR (Corporate Social Responsibility) activities results in an increased number of such cooperation with the education system.

B., a representative of the high-tech company described the measures taken within the framework of CSR which he promotes in the organization:

> A decision was made to invest in three topics: A. STEM; B. Inclusion of women, peripherals, Arabs, etc. We think how to increase the percentage [of their participation in the labor market]; C. Transformation Technology which means technology which makes transformation. Take, for example, the Waze app that changed our lives … So as a corporation, we need to make it happen.

6.3.4 Strategic Risk 4: Sectoral Gaps

Two courses of action are suggested (Courses of action 12 and 13) for coping with this risk.

Course of action 12: Established cooperation with for-profit and nonprofit organizations

As noted, in the last decade, NGOs, both for-profit and nonprofit organizations, have become involved in STEM education in different ways of government-NGOs relations: from rivalry and competition, through contract-based cooperation relationships, to cooperation and collaboration (Coston 1998). However, procedural barriers have been identified that inhibit the efficiency of these processes.

In order to deal with the tension between control (by the education system) and privatization (outsourcing to external bodies) of education, the *institutionalized cooperation* pattern of inter-sectoral cooperation is proposed (Schiffer et al. 2010). Within this pattern of operation, the education system manages the second and third sectors' involvement in the education system by decentralization. This kind of cooperation protects the education system position as a public system, but also allows other sectors to act autonomously, based on the understanding of their unique contribution to the education system.

The study participants often presented contradicting positions. On one side, a position that objects the privatization of education and emphasizes the need to return the control of the education system to the Ministry of Education, is heard, as is described by A., a representative of the academia:

> The introduction of extra-school programs into the school is very bad. If I was the Minister of Education, I would say that I lost control of the education system, give me back the keys. It is not a realistic situation that a principal would be busy all day with the integration of different factors, to change curriculum every five years because the NGOs want… The education system has lost its leading position because of such things.

And, on the other hand, an approach which stresses the importance of cooperation with all agencies was proposed, as an opportunity to close social gaps and as a means to achieve the goals of STEM education. In other words, in order to allow nonprofit and for-profit organizations to help in the reduction of social gaps and to increase the representation of underrepresented sectors in STEM studies, the Ministry of Education must lead the cooperation in terms of managing multi-sectoral relationships with multiple actors (O'Leary and Vij 2012). Such partnership recognizes the need of the education system to collaborate with agencies characterized by high flexibility concerning budget issues.

In both cases, it is important to realize that the state is only one element in a network of policy makers, and therefore must deal with an array of dependencies involving public and private resources.

Course of action 13: Inclusion of sectors which are partly represented in STEM education

The shortage of practical engineers, engineers, and other employees with technical skills exhibited recently in Israel, is conveyed by the risk factors which address the need for a continuity in the curricula (see Chap. 4—Study sequences). These shortages elevate the need for increasing number of graduates of STEM education. At the same time, many social sectors are not represented in STEM studies in the high school relatively to their size in the population, and accordingly, their representation in the IDF, the academy and the labor market is significantly low.

The research participants address the importance of the cross-sectoral cooperation as a tool for:

- reducing the representation gaps of students from socially and economically peripheral in STEM studies at the advanced level;
- encouraging female students to select STEM studies;
- increasing the participation in STEM studies among students from the ultra-orthodox sector (mainly male students who do not study science at all in the school);
- promoting the representation of the Arab sector in high school STEM education that may increase its representation in the Israeli industry in accordance with its share in the population.

In a focus group in an Arab community high school, participants raised the importance of including a study program that addresses employment options as well as academic opportunities for STEM graduates that will encourage students to choose these subjects:

> The state should offer a program for the integration of students from weak sectors as employees in the future labor market. This will strongly reinforce the technology education tracks.

With respect to male ultraorthodox students, who do not learn science and technology at all, it was suggested to encourage them to start studying STEM subjects at a later age. A graduate student of the ultraorthodox education system, explained:

> I have extensive experience with ultra-orthodox schools and yeshiva students who at a relatively older age (18-22) turn to the scientific world (with preparatory courses and then in universities or colleges). The gap is reduced in a very short time and [they] succeed… We should offer them this option [to study] and encourage as many of them to choose this way.

This deliberate policy of the education system, of expanding cooperation in educational projects in which students from underrepresented groups in STEM education study, may reduce social gaps. In this spirit, many educational initiatives that reflect cooperation of different stakeholders are operated today. The number of these initiatives has been increased since 2012, when the Ministry of Education announced a strategic plan to strengthen STEM education in Israel (Ministry of Education 2012).

As an evidence for the volume of activities, we list initiatives that aim to reduce the gender gap, by encouraging female students to select STEM subjects, which are, in fact, some form of cooperation of the education system, academia, industry, and the IDF: TWIST,[8] "Future Female Scientists"[9] and "Leading to the Technion in Science, Industry, Technology and Engineering."[10]

6.4 Cross-Sector Collaboration in Risk Management of STEM Education

The response plan highlights the cooperation of the stakeholders in the risk management process of STEM education in Israel as a way to mitigate strategic risks. These positions of the study participants' reflects the fact that more and more organizations, both for-profit and nonprofit, cooperate with the education system in different forms: development of educational content in STEM education, implementation of projects in science and technology in secondary schools, budget assistance, construction of educational technology centers, etc.

Such forms of cooperation are desired also from the perspective of the education system. Dr. Ofer Rimon, Head of the Science and Technology Administration at the Ministry of Education, presented this perspective at the Knesset Committee of Science and Technology in 2015 in a discussion on STEM education:

> Many of our partners are sitting here around the table. The technology chain of school, the Manufacturers Association, the professional unions, the IDF, which … is the first professional organization that our students, many of them, meet. So we are closely coordinated with the IDF.

So far, we can learn that opportunities for cross-sectoral organization exist, when the risks are managed by the system of STEM education. However, alongside the desire for cooperation, weaknesses were also emphasized in the cooperative work with the education system. The research participants, representatives of for-profit and nonprofits organizations, whose activities are limited by contract with the education system, pointed to bureaucratic processes and expressed the desire to cooperate in professional decisions-making and not just being their operators.

Thus, the study's findings indicate the need to examine optimal ways to involve the stakeholders of STEM education and cooperate with them in STEM education processes.

The research findings specified the *institutionalized cooperation* (Schiffer et al. 2010) as the preferable collaboration pattern. This pattern of cooperation enables to create an infrastructure for joint activities, when the education system is the

---

[8]The program website: http://www.mada.org.il/culture/twist, http://www.the-twist-project.eu/en/.

[9]The program website: http://most.gov.il/ScienceAndCommunity/futurescientist/Pages/default.aspx.

[10]The program website: http://www.movilot-latechnion.com/about_u/.

responsible agent for what goes inside the education system, while the second and third sector organizations operate through philanthropic assistance in fields which are determined by the education system. In the implementation process of this pattern of collaboration, a regulation system is established that preserves the power balance in favor of the education system.

However, this type of partnership does not provide freedom to the second and third sectors in determining the educational content. In practice, the education system is the body which initiates the creation of new programs and is just assisted by the second and third sectors with their implementation. In addition, the education system operates control mechanisms over the partners' activities to ensure maximum efficiency of the allocated budget.

Johnston et al. (2011) explain that successful collaborative governance is reflected in a climate that fosters trust, mutual responsibility, and a willingness to share risks. The stakeholders are required to trust each other for a long term, which is a profound conceptual change that may take place only in an open and trustworthy environment. This idea is further developed by the economist Robert Reich (the Minister of Labor of the United States under Bill Clinton administration) in general, and in the Israeli context by Tamir (2015). These ideas present a new public dialogue. A dialogue that reflects the society's desire to reduce social gaps for the benefit of everyone. If the public conception will undergo a conceptual change process and the second and third sectors will operate as ideal philanthropy,[11] different or other collaboration patterns may fit.

For example, in the case discussed in this Brief, stakeholders' cooperation for the mitigation of the strategic risks may be more efficient if the cooperation will also transfer the responsibility. Examples for such a process are the proposed courses of action for dealing with the salaries of STEM teachers: "STEM teachers' mobility" (Course of action 3) and "Integrated earning" (Course of action 5). These actions suggest the recruiting of the industry and the education system to enable STEM teachers to be engaged in both occupations at the same time and to allow teachers' mobility between sectors. If the responsibility of managing this process had been transferred to the stakeholders, and the cooperation was not perceived as help provided to the education system to "solve" its problems, the process might have been more effective.

Recently, the Israeli Ministry of Education leads a process that examines its relationships and partnerships that exist today with the second and third sectors and with higher education institutions. The target is to optimize the procedure of inter-sectoral collaboration. The documentation of the civic society organization "Shitufim,"[12] which accompanies this process, indicates a unique procedure performed consistently during the last two years with full transparency of contents and knowledge. The process is led by the Ministry of Education and it is evident that it

[11]Ideal philanthropy is an altruistic approach that focuses on the contribution to social needs that are not provided by the government.

[12]Shitufim website: http://www.sheatufim.org.il/.

expresses a desire to delineate clear coordination mechanisms for inter-sectors cooperation. The CEO of the Ministry of Education, Mrs. Michal Cohen, expressed this view, in the following quote documented in a meeting with all the partners in October 2015:

> The current process, which deals with coordination mechanisms, seeks to produce cooperative governance of the Ministry of Education, by connecting strategic planning processes, by which the office operates, and actual works, by using cross-sectoral partnerships which are involved in the course of action, along the annual planning program. … It is expected to see the implementation of the programs as part of long-term collaborative governance regardless specific policy makers and role holders.

Her words may indicate the desire to establish an institutionalized cooperation between all stakeholders of STEM education in Israel.

6.5 Summary

In this chapter, we presented the response plan for the mitigation of the strategic risks of STEM education in Israel identified in the first phase of the risk management process and ranted in the second phase.

The response plan heavily relies on the cooperation between sectors and stakeholders. Though we do not recommend to implement a specific cooperation pattern, it is recommended to choose an inter-sectoral cooperation style that allows the establishment of relationships that ensure continued cooperation process, which lays out a clear policy for the partnership implementation based on trust relationships. Nevertheless, it is essential to regulate the partnership guidelines due to the increase number of third sector organizations working in the field of education in recent decades. This policy concerns education researchers (e.g., Michaeli 2010) who view this phenomenon as a threat to STEM education.

References

Ben Israel, Y & Kuns, N. (2013). Risk management according to Ben Gurion's approach, *Maarachot (Systems)* 452, 32–37 (Hebrew).

Coston, J. M. (1998). A model and typology of government-NGO relationships. *Nonprofit and Voluntary Sector Quarterly* 27(3), 358–382.

Deci, E. L. & Ryan, R. M. (2008). Hedonia, eudaimonia, and well-being: An introduction, *Journal of Happiness Studies* **9**(1), 1–11.

European commission. (2013). Key Data on Teachers and School Leaders in Europe. http://eacea.ec.europa.eu/education/eurydice/documents/key_data_series/151EN.pdf.

Hanhijoki, I., Katajisto, J., Kimari, M., & Savioja, H. (2012). Education, training and demand for labour in Finland by 2025. http://www.oph.fi/download/144754_Education_training_and_demand_for_labour_in_Finland_by_2025_2.pdf.

Hillson, D. (2001). Effective strategies for exploiting opportunities. In *Proceedings of the 32nd Annual Project Management Institute Seminars & Symposium (PMI 2001)*, Nashville US, 5–7.

IRM (2002). *Risk Management Standard*. The Institute of Risk Management (IRM), The Association of Insurance and Risk Managers (AIRMIC) and the National Forum for Risk Management in the Public Sector (ALARM). https://www.theirm.org/media/886059/ARMS_2002_IRM.pdf.

Johnston, E. W., Hicks, D., Nan, N., & Auer, J. C. (2011). Managing the inclusion process in collaborative governance. *Journal of Public Administration Research and Theory* 21(4), 699–721.

Michaeli, N. (2010). Privatization processes in the Israeli education system. MASA – A portal on teaching and teacher training. http://portal.macam.ac.il/ArticlePage.aspx?id=3221.

Mikes, A. & Kaplan, R. S. (2014). *Towards a contingency theory of enterprise risk management*. Harvard Business School.

Ministry of Education (2012). Preparing the Future Leadership in Science and Technology, http://cms.education.gov.il/NR/rdonlyres/E0B8F780-137D-4785-969D-208790D983E6/124762/av16022011.pdf.

OECD. (2015). *Education at a Glance 2015 OECD Indicators*. http://meyda.education.gov.il/files/MinhalCalcala/EAG2015.pdf.

O'Leary, R., & Vij, N. (2012). Collaborative public management: Where have we been and where are we going?. *The American Review of Public Administration*, 0275074012445780.

Oplatka, Y. (2007). The Foundations of Education Administration: Leadership and Management in the Educational Organization, Pardes Publications (Hebrew).

Sahlberg, P. (2011). *Finnish Lessons*, the series of school reform.

Schiffer, V., Berkovitz, Y., Bar-Yehuda, S., & Almog-Bareket, G. (2010). *The Involvement of Third Sector Organizations in the Education system – White Paper*, Van-Leer Institute, Jerusalem (Hebrew). http://www.vanleer.org.il/sites/files/product-pdf/73-sFileRedir.pdf.

Tamir, Y. (2015). *Who's Afraid of Equality? On Education and Society in Israel*, Yediot Achronot, Hemed Books.

Weissblei, I. (2013). *National Councils of Education – A Comparison Review*, The Knesset Center for Research and Information, Jerusalem. http://www.knesset.gov.il/MMM/data/pdf/m03263.pdf (Hebrew).

Chapter 7
What Can STEM Education Systems in the World Learn from the Israeli Case?

Abstract This Brief illustrates the application of a full risk management process for an education system—STEM education in Israel. We hope that this description illustrates the suitability of risk management processes also for educational organization. In this chapter, we suggest conceptual ideas that stood behind the methodological risk management process we applied in our study. We hope that these guidelines as well will be useful for other nations, which realize lately the importance of STEM education as a basic knowledge required for all their K-12 graduates.

Keywords Risk management · STEM education · Conceptual ideas · International readership · K-12 education · Meta-practices · MERge model · Internal dimensions · External dimensions

7.1 Meta-Practices of Risk Management

In this chapter, we suggest the following conceptual ideas that stood behind the methodological risk management process we applied in our study. Since no hierarchy exists between them, they are presented in an alphabetically order.

Acknowledge the importance of STEM education. Any knowledge at any level in the STEM subjects will give children a competitive advantage in their future professional lives. By a competitive advantage we do not advocate competition; to the contrary: the more skills a person has, the more he or she tends to collaborate in order to exhaust these skills more meaningfully and efficiently. Therefore, in line with the value of diversity (see below), in order to allow each child to find his or her the adequate professional development path, basic STEM education should be provided.

Adopt a *MERge* perspective (Hazzan and Lis-Hacohen 2016). The *MERge* perspective advocates that practitioners should have three meta-skills: Management, Education, and Research to successfully exhaust and promote their professional

A. Even Zahav and O. Hazzan, *Risk Management of Education Systems*,
SpringerBriefs in Education, DOI 10.1007/978-3-319-51984-5_7

development. Clearly, these three meta-skills were largely expressed in the risk management process of STEM education in Israel, as described in this Brief.

Be agile. Agility means many things. In the case of STEM education, we propose to adopt the agile idea of setting long-term targets and then achieving them in small and gradual steps. These small steps should be accompanied with a careful examination of the results of each step, in order to plan and apply the next steps wisely.

Be open, talk about problems. Without admitting the problems, problems can neither be located nor treated.

Be proactive. Proactivity means that a practitioner does not wait till a problem starts effecting the results of his or her organization, but rather, looks ahead, plans the future, and acts methodologically toward its accomplishment. This approach is totally different from the reactive approach, which guides practitioners to wait till a problem emerges, and then start analyzing its source and trying to fix it. The risk management process described in this Brief illustrates how a *proactive* approach can also be adopted in the public sector in general and in education systems in particular.

Enable each child to exhaust his or her potential. This idea should be considered as one of the basic principles of risk management processes conducted in educational systems and organizations. In practice, on the individual level, as soon as it is recognized that a child needs a special learning environment, because he or she is either gifted or face some other challenges, in the proactive spirit of risk management, this need should be treated in one of the suggested strategies for risk management processes (Sect. 2.4).

Give top priority to teachers' voice. Many reports, which discuss the topic of education from different perspectives, are published without including the teachers' opinions. Furthermore, in many cases, teaches are not invited to serve in committees, which deal with subjects that teachers are the experts about them. Clearly, this situation is unaccepted and should be changed.

Increase diversity and inclusion. As our community becomes more diverse and multicultural, it is essential to inspire the values of inclusion and diversity in any educational program in general, and programs that plan for the future, as is done in risk management processes, in particular.

Increase teacher autonomy. This guideline stresses the need to give teachers the academic freedom in order to accomplish their job targets successfully. It should be remembered that, as professionals, teachers are *the* experts about teaching.

Share responsibility of the education system with different sectors. The risk management analysis presented in this Brief reflects a multi-faceted perspective on STEM education that is not limited to educational lens. Due to the inclusion of stakeholders from different sectors in our study, it was possible to elicit a wide perspective at the risks with which STEM education in Israel faces, wider than any sector by itself could have been produced.

Use wisdom generated, collected, and gathered in other domains. Such a wide perspective allows to learn from other kinds of organizations, cultures, societies, and disciplines. In our era, the ability to learn from so many resources, beyond our immediate zone, should be exhausted intensively.

7.2 Summary

This Brief suggests to implement risk management processes in STEM education in general and on the national level in particular. We note that though the focus was placed on STEM education, the *technology* has not been identified as a risk by the different stakeholders. Further, the risk categories did not address what happens in the school in general—e.g., organizational structure, teaching load, teacher teamwork, etc. This observation is interesting since in many cases when an education system is examined, part of the attention is directed toward these *internal* factors. Accordingly, we suggest that the approach proposed in this Brief has the potential to add new and *external* dimensions—such as proactive approach, global perspective, and cross-sector collaboration—with respect to the analysis of education systems in general and the promotion of STEM education in particular.

Reference

Hazzan, O., & Lis-Hacohen, R. (2016). *The MERge Model for Business Development: The Amalgamation of Management, Education and* Research, SpringerBriefs in Business. http://www.springer.com/us/book/9783319302249

FSC
www.fsc.org
MIX
Papier | Fördert
gute Waldnutzung
FSC® C083411

Kolibri 360 GmbH
Ferdinand-Jühlke-Straße 7
99095 Erfurt, Deutschland
produktsicherheit@kolibri360.de